OBJEKT©INTERNATIONAL

highlights of international luxury

OBJEKT©INTERNATIONAL

highlights of international luxury

photographed by Hans Fonk

ART

DESIGN

ARCHITECTURE

AND

FUN

AROUND

THE WORLD

teNeues

CONTENTS

FOREWORD

Meeting Hans Fonk is a serendipitous event!

On the surface, he is a good looking gentleman; quiet most times, but able to give a winning smile that is full of enthusiasm, charm, and wit! No wonder his magazine OBJEKT©International reflects his personality. But, in addition, the magazine brings to the reader a wide array of international, original interiors hardly seen in other media!

Somehow, this "pirate" finds treasures in all four corners of the world, and then captures the spirit of every nuance in each interior and presents it to his readers who are addicted to OBJEKT©International—one of the most luxurious magazines in the entire world.
Every architect should be lucky enough to have his work captured through the lens of Hans Fonk. Same way with the interiors which always look spectacular and dramatic!

By luxurious, I mean the good taste, discretion he uses in cropping pictures properly, and with originality. The angles he shoots from, and the overall layout throughout is beyond normal expectations, and way above the standards design and architecture readers are accustomed to see.

Hans Fonk incessantly travels all 4 corners of the world and finds subjects that are so unique, settings that are so outstanding, and angles that only his critical eye and lens can see!
In spite of his wide travels and hectic schedule, he manages to throw in a bunch of wit and tender moments and conversations that prove that Hans is thinking and working with his heart!

This book reflects that: it is a compilation of the photos and productions he has made for OBJEKT©International in recent years.

George M. Beylerian

DAVID BEATON'S
MUSKOKA COTTAGE PARADISE

The boathouse and cottage are on an island in Lake Joseph, one of the three lakes known as the Muskoka
Lakes, north of the Canadian city of Toronto. Here cottage culture reigns supreme. David Beaton and his wife
Heather have created their nautical El Dorado that matches perfectly with the natural surroundings.
The structure houses two classic sport boats plus a modern Chris-Craft.
And Beaton has three more fast boats moored alongside the surrounding decks.

Left: The Beatons' boathouse. The cottage itself nestles among the trees at a higher level. Both the cottage and the boathouse are built of wood and in such a way that they form a natural part of the imposing surroundings.

Above: One of the Beatons' two classic boats in the boathouse. It is a Hacker Craft built in 1982. These boats were the brainchild of John L. Hacker, who started building mahogany sport boats, runabouts, and racers at the end of the 19th century. A handmade Hacker Craft was soon to become the most desirable vessel for celebrities and captains of industry. Today the company is still building boats of 20 to 42 feet using the founder's original designs. Hacker is located at Silver Bay, New York.

Left: Heather and David Beaton on board one of their yachts, a Pursuit, on Lake Joseph. The lake is one of the "big three" Muskoka lakes north of Toronto. This El Dorado has countless traditional and less traditional cottages, many of which have their own boathouses
Right: The cottage seen from the island with a Dedon swing in the foreground.

Muskoka Lakes are a two-hours' drive north of the Canadian city of Toronto. It is a vast area with over 1600 lakes, the jewels in the crown being Lake Muskoka, Lake Joseph, and Lake Rosseau. At the beginning of the 20th century these three lakes were "discovered" primarily by wealthy Americans who built their holiday cottages and boathouses there.

Luxury hotels like the Royal Muskoka, the Windermere, and Elgin House soon attracted the nobility and the wealthy from Europe and North America. A cottage of one's own beside one of the three lakes, was considered the norm for optimum enjoyment, and as you sail on these lakes, it's easy to understand why. In the second half of the last century, the area was dubbed the Hollywood of the north, because film stars and directors like Goldie Hawn, Kurt Russell, Martin Short, Steven Spielberg, and Tom Hanks liked to visit or had their own cottages there.

It's an earthly paradise: the three lakes dotted with rocky islands that are adorned with wild vegetation comprising mainly of pine trees. In the center of this El Dorado is Port Carling. It has a number of boatyards where they build and restore classic boats.

Here on Lake Joseph (or Lake Joe as it is called by those in the know) Heather and David Beaton built their cottage, the aim being to have it blend into the surroundings as much as possible.

"In 1990 I came here and eventually found a cottage to let. In 2002 I was able to buy this bit of island in Lake Joe. It's been the most desirable lake for a cottage for years. This was an undeveloped piece of land with mainly pine trees growing on it. There we were with our dog," David said.

He soon had an area levelled out and went on to build a wooden cottage on it. Each year he made improvements and in 2005 the time was ripe to build a boathouse, or at least the section at water level. Three years later they added a storey for use as guest accommodation. Everything is timber here. The form and the color of both cottage and boathouse have been selected to blend into the natural surroundings.
In 2010 or thereabouts all the "wooden paddle stuff" was thrown out and the boathouse was fitted out to accommodate accessories for the deluxe brands he represents in Canada. Below there are three boats bobbing around and on the upper level there is a living room, an al fresco dining area and a bedroom. All the spaces open onto a large deck running round the building. "We come out here as soon as we have some spare time. We entertain here and we often bring along clients. It's become part of our showroom," David explained.

These pages
Above: A view of the guest quarters on the first floor with a teak sofa by Roda, wooden elements by Riva, and chairs by McGuire. In the bedroom, an E15 bed, chairs by McGuire, and a Baker console. In the passage accessing the bedroom, double doors open onto the covered al fresco dining area with Dedon furniture designed by Philippe Starck. The bedroom has a panoramic view over part of Lake Joseph and the islands where moose, bears, and deer roam free.
Below: The boathouse at Lake Joseph one of the Muskoka Lakes north of Toronto. The boathouse is furnished with furniture by Roda and Dedon. The boat in the foreground is a Pursuit. In the background, one of the two Boston Whalers from Beaton's armada.

He's a good talker and it's hardly surprising he followed his friends' advice and became a salesman. But no ordinary salesman—one with flair and style. Success didn't just fall into his lap. Having worked in an aircraft factory and having partied for a year at college, he embarked on selling extremely cheap furniture from a van that he had to push start himself.

When he came in contact with Sitag of Switzerland he soon realized he would do much better to import top interior brands. The Swiss work ethic also became his guiding light. Vitra was his first major brand—until then it was almost unknown in Canada. He saw opportunities where others hesitated and he was prepared to take risks. Business took off then and his company was to become a household name in North America. In 1997 he opened an office furniture showroom in Toronto.
He discovered that a lot of the furniture was being sold for residential use, so in 1999 he opened "studio b" which is geared more to private clients, and combines such brands as Walter Knoll, Baker, Dedon, McGuire, Baccarat, and Barbara Barry under that name successfully. With "plan b" he acquired leading brands like Vitra, Herman Miller, Fritz Hansen, Technogym, Lapalma, Meridiani, Anta Lights, Glatz, and Roda. And his clientele includes W Hotels, Four Seasons Hotels and Resorts, Fairmont Hotels and Resorts, BMW, Volkswagen, Mercedes-Benz, Audi, Hugo Boss, FMC Law, Goodmans, and Gowlings.

He comments in that respect: "A lot of willpower and a focus on luxury and quality were the deciding factors. There's always a market for luxury. There's only one right way to do things and that's to focus on the luxury brands you work with. Be loyal to those brands and stand by them." Today all his activities are concentrated in Toronto. When traffic isn't too heavy, it takes him just over two hours to reach Muskoka.

The boathouse fits three boats inside. In the foreground the Beaton's SeaBirD, built in 1956 by Port Carling Boatworks. On the right there is a Chris-Craft pre-owned by actress Goldie Hawn who also has a lakeside cottage here.
This SeaBirD is Heather's favourite vessel for cruising the lakes. Boats like this are part of the Muskoka Lake heritage, as are the traditionally built cottages and boathouses. Many of them were built in the village Port Carling, located between the three big lakes Muskoka, Joseph, and Rosseau. It is home to a number of boatworks that specialize in building and restoring classic sport boats and runabouts.
Port Carling Boatworks started building such crafts back in 1925. A fire in 1931 destroyed large areas of Port Carling, including the boatyard. After it was rebuilt it was to focus on producing SeaBirDs. During the Second World War the company built 25-foot cutters for the Royal Canadian Navy. The last SeaBirD was built in 1958.

Next pages:
Old and new mix well on the Muskoka lakes.
Left: a modern Chris-Craft, an American specialist in fast boats with an impressive boating history. The company that is now referred to as Chris-Craft, was started on Point du Chene, in Algonac, Michigan, a small town on the St. Clair River. It was here that Christopher Columbus Smith built his first boat in 1874 at age 13. Since that time, the boatbuilder's main passion was speed.
Right: The SeaBirD from 1956.

Above: In Fort Worth in the state of Texas, USA, the Japanese architect Tadao Ando designed the Modern Art Museum. It is, in itself, an architectural artwork. Three pavilions with vast cantilevered roofs in concrete seem to float in the pool.
Left: The taut museum façade with a glazed "cut-out" forming the front entrance.

TADAO ANDO'S
ARCHITECTURAL PURITY

The building, in its very simplicity, possesses extraordinary purity. The form, the massive planar

walls in smooth concrete, and the visible architectural structure make of it a modern work of art.

This is the Modern Art Museum designed by the Japanese architect, Tadao Ando.

It is situated in the Cultural District of Forth Worth, Texas.

A building of lasting beauty, it comprises various large open spaces and

pavilions which seem to float in a vast pool.

Above: The entrance lobby with large, glass curtain walls on either side adding a feeling of great transparency to the space.
Bottom left: The elliptically shaped restaurant that stands in the water. Bottom right: An exhition pavillion with a work by Felix Gonzalez-Torres, *Untitled LA, 1991* from The Rachofsky Collection.
Next: One of the pavilions seen from the entrance lobby with *L'Etrusco* (1976) by Italian artist Michelangelo Pistoletto.

Fort Worth's Cultural District is situated on the outskirts of the city. It is a concentration of museums, including the Kimbell Art Museum designed by Louis Kahn, the Museum of Science and History by Legorreta + Legorreta Architects and Philip Johnson's Amon Carter Center.

The Modern Art Museum is surely the simplest and purest architectural work, and, therefore, the most impactful. It is architecture with no need of a story; it clothes subtlety and simplicity in powerful forms and striking materials like concrete, glass and steel. The stark, rectangular concrete façade has, at its center, a large glazed opening housing the front entrance. Behind the glass curtain wall, framed in metal, there is a vast lobby and, on the other side, an equally high transparent glass wall overlooking the artificial pool, in which three pavilions appear to float. Beyond the water feature, there is a sculpture garden. The lobby is tall and long, and rests on concrete pillars, which guarantee maximum transparency. Unpretentious concrete benches reinforce the feeling of space.

On one side Ando has made room for a large art work, plus a mezzanine floor above. A narrow corridor, again with a high window wall, leads past the pool to the circular shaped restaurant that stands in the water.

On the other side of the entrance lobby is the actual entrance to the exhibition spaces. There, stairs access a conveniently-ordered succession of galleries, where changing exhibitions and the museum's permanent collection are displayed under the soft light entering through linear skylights. The permanent collection contains over 3,000 works by a wide range of artists including Anselm Kiefer, Robert Motherwell, Pablo Picasso, Jackson Pollock, Gerhard Richter, Susan Rothenberg, Richard Serra, Andres Serrano, Cindy Sherman, and Andy Warhol.

Striking features in the complex are the three tall pavilions situated in the water with their immense cantilevered roofs which shield the artworks from direct daylight.

In remarks on his work, the architect wrote:
"I try to relate the fixed form and compositional method to the kind of life that will be lived in the given space and to local regional society. My mainstay in selecting the solutions to these problems is my independent architectural theory ordered on the basis of a geometry of simple forms, my own ideas of life, and my emotions as a Japanese."

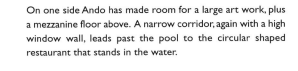

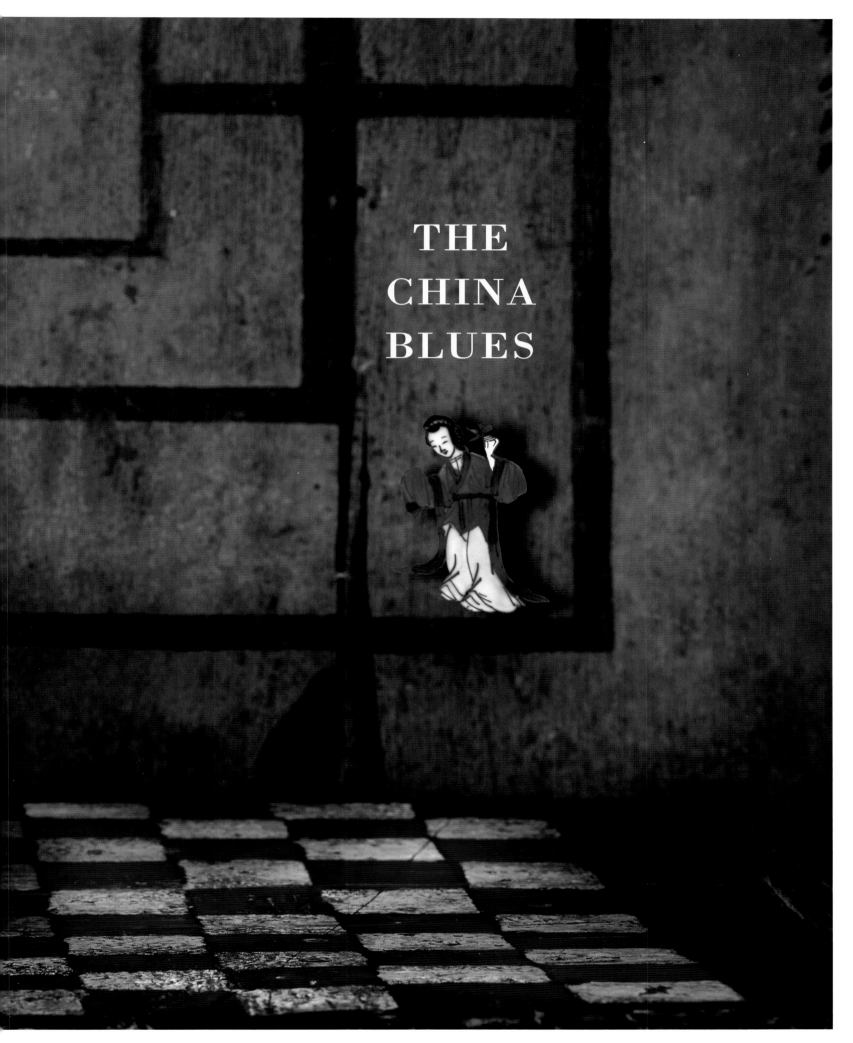

THE CHINA BLUES

At an auction at Sotheby's, a buyer paid over $ 38 million for

a Ming Dynasty wine cup.

In recent years, massive attendance at auctions of

Oriental art–and the prices the items command–

confirms that interest is greater than ever,

particularly in Chinese antiques.

Since the 17th century, the Netherlands has a key position

in the trading of fine Chinese porcelain.

Previous pages:
Two square, blue-and-white Chinese vases with geometric pattern; h. 17.5 cm. Date: c. 1670.

Above: Chinese jar from the Yuan dynasty (1279-1368), h. 27.5 cm. It was auctioned in London in 2005 and fetched US $27,679,100–until recently, the highest price ever paid at auction for a work of Asian art.
Next page clockwise from top left: A ribbed knob vase, h. 23 cm. The decoration is of precious objects in a medallion. Kangxi period. Beside that: the base of the Kangxi bowl (which is decorated with a continuous scene of figures in a landscape and interior) has a 6-character mark within in a double ring, which indicates the best quality. Date: c. 1700. Bottom right: A Kangxi-period jug with floral decoration. The model is derived from Persian types. Height: 15 cm.
The two large dishes are Wanli period *kraak* porcelain, diam. c. 29.5 cm. Date: 1580-1600. Generally the back of typical *kraak* porcelain pieces has minimal decoration. The octagonal medallion on the front shows a bird in a landscape. On the reversed saucer, a Wan Li *klapmuts* bowl (diam. 14 cm), also dating from the late 16th century.

Auctions of Chinese porcelain are nothing new. Back in 1602 and 1604 over a hundred thousand pieces, seized from the Portuguese, were auctioned in Amsterdam and Middelburg. The buyers even included representatives of the English and French courts who readily paid astronomical sums for the goods. The Portuguese had introduced the extremely rare blue-and-white porcelain into Europe in the sixteenth century. Dutch middlemen bought it in Antwerp and Lisbon, and sold it in Holland. But after 1594 it was not possible to trade with the Portuguese, as Holland and Portugal were at war and Dutch ships were refused entry into Portuguese ports. No longer was porcelain purchased from the Portuguese, but seized as booty.

After the cargo of the Portuguese merchant ship the San Jago had been auctioned in 1602, the Netherlands assumed a key position in the import and trading of the much sought-after Chinese porcelain. The founding in that year of the Dutch East India Company resulted in a highly lucrative monopoly position, which was to last for almost two centuries.
The oldest Chinese export porcelain is called in Dutch *kraak*, probably named after the *carraca* (carrack)—the Portuguese merchant ships that transported it. *Kraak* porcelain, made during the latter period of the Ming dynasty, is often characterised by panels with blue decorations along the rim or the side of the item. This export ware, named after the Chinese emperor Wan Li, can be roughly dated between 1560 and the first quarter of the 17th century–the final period of the Ming dynasty. Decorative motifs include flowers, birds, deer, horses, and Chinese figures.

Kraak porcelain is relatively finely-bodied and is painted under a glaze that is porous in places. The glaze on the inner side of the ring foot is often rough to the touch on account of the sand grit that adhered to the object during firing. Unlike Chinese porcelain of a later date, *kraak* porcelain very rarely bears marks on the back.

In the Netherlands a great deal of Chinese porcelain was to be found in the highly desirable art and curiosities collections assembled by the elite in the 16th and 17th centuries.
For instance, an inventory drawn up in 1634 of the collection of Amelia van Solms (the stadholder's spouse) at her palace in The Hague lists over 550 pieces of Oriental porcelain. And many a 17th-century *pronk* (ostentation) still-life depicts expensive *kraak* porcelain.

Demand for the exotic product increased year by year. From the mid-17th century the production method was perfected and the porcelain being made at that time was termed transition ware.
Porcelain decorators had then adopted a freer style, because they were no longer bound by the strict rules of the imperial court. New shapes and decorations were introduced and the Chinese town of Jingdezhen became the main center for the production of blue-and-white decorated porcelain. Yet most of the kilns were destroyed during internal wars, meaning that the production and export of porcelain stagnated for several decades.
It was not until the reign of emperor Kangxi (1662-1722) that the wrecked imperial kilns were rebuilt and production (and export to Europe) were resumed. That heralded a period of prosperity in which high-quality porcelain was being produced: extremely delicate and bright white ware, with an underglaze decoration varying from pale to deep sapphire blue. The pieces were decorated with flowers, landscapes, gardens, female figures, dignitaries, children at play, Chinese interiors, symbolical themes or motifs customized for the West. Moreover, there was a demand for European styles. Western pewter, wood, glass, and silver objects were shipped to China, with the request that they be copied in porcelain.
And so porcelain tea caddies, salt cellars, candlesticks, tankards, and numerous items of dinnerware were made, to give cachet to the tables and parlors of the European elite.

Left: Étagere vase, h. 6 cm, Kangxi period, with depiction of a Chinese lady (known as Lange Lijs or Long Eliza). Date: 1662-1722.
Above: An étagere vase with a depiction of a Chinese lady and plants in a pot; c. 1700. The openwork handles contain two small porcelain rings. Total height: 7.6 cm.

In the course of the 18th century the hype around blue-and-white decorated porcelain gradually waned. Partly because the quality of the product was dropping, but also because European customers preferred the fashionable polychrome-painted porcelain. Moreover, porcelain was also being made in Europe by that time. And the home-grown variety proved to be easier to order and cheaper than the Chinese export porcelain.

After all, European manufacturers were quite able to zero in quickly on changing trends in the 18th-century interior. Thanks to the fact that services of better-quality Chinese porcelain were seldom for everyday use and had been handled with care since the early 17th century, a relatively large amount has remained in the Netherlands undamaged. Antique Chinese porcelain is not really rare, because over the centuries, thousands of shiploads must have travelled from China to the West and sold here.

By way of illustration: every shipment consisted of 150,000 pieces, though almost half would arrive broken at their destination. Nevertheless, it is safe to say that over time millions of porcelain objects must have made their way to Europe—at least, when the ship, and its fragile cargo, did not sink on the return voyage.

Nowadays, private collectors and museum curators even travel from the Far East to attend auctions in the Netherlands, where they acquire their antique porcelain, which is very hard to find in the country where it originated.

The Amsterdam branch of Christie's auction house has built up an international reputation for organizing important auctions of recently recovered cargoes from shipwrecks.

For instance, they auctioned more than 25,000 items of Ming and Transition porcelain found in a Chinese junk that sank around 1640. In addition, the auction of in excess of 150,000 porcelain objects from the cargo of the VOC ship (East-Indiaman) *Geldermalsen*, which sank in 1752, attracted buyers from all over the world and produced record proceeds for porcelain, which was not of particularly exceptional quality and had suffered from centuries of abrasion from seawater and sand.

Evidently the adventurous salvaging of ancient wrecks and their valuable cargoes appeals to everyone's imagination and, accordingly, buyers attribute added value to porcelain originating from specific cargoes.

Leila de Vos van Steenwijk, head of the Asian Art department at Christie's recalled: "Since 1973 we have organized a dozen or so auctions featuring an entire cargo of antique porcelain. And, without exception, the proceeds surpassed the pre-sale estimates. In addition, we hold auctions twice a year in Amsterdam devoted explicitly to Asian art.

Obviously Oriental porcelain forms a major part of the items offered. The market is booming and recording growing interest from Asian buyers in particular.

There they want undamaged—and preferably early—export porcelain with decoration in the Chinese taste. Over the years, I must have handled thousands of objects that have meanwhile found their way into private and museum collections worldwide."

"But sometimes you encounter something that is truly unique. For example, Hetty von der Gablentz—senior director of Christie's—and I discovered a piece belonging to a private

Above: Miniature porcelain cups and saucers decorated with bass and water plants. The saucers are 6 cm in diameter, the cups are 2.6 cm in height. Kangxi period: early 18th century.
Right: Various small etagere vases dating from the Kangxi period (1662-1722).
The trolley model front left measures 5.8 cm. Miniature vases of this type became very popular in the course of the 18th century because they could be displayed in the showcase doll houses belonging to the gentry.

Dutch owner: an unusual blue-and-white decorated jar, which at first sight appeared to date from the Ming period. Yes, our job is full of excitement. When we did the research that item proved to be an extremely rare piece from the Yuan dynasty (1279-1368). And we know of only eight such jars in the world. The provenance was exciting too: a Dutch baron, captain Haro van Hemert, who was in the Dutch Navy and stationed in China from 1913 to 1923, was an avid collector of antique porcelain. He must have purchased this jar (27.5 cm in height and 33 cm in diameter) locally in China."

It goes without saying that beneficiaries of Van Hemert's estate were more than pleasantly surprised by the astronomical figure of more than $27.6 million ultimately fetched by this unique find. It was at that time the most expensive work of Asian art ever to be sold. The previous record for a piece of porcelain was held by a pilgrim flask from the Yuan period, sold in 2003 in New York for $5.8 million .

In 2010 Sotheby's sold a Gourd Qianlong vase for $32,4 million and in 2014 a small Ming Dynasty-Cheng Hua period Chicken Wine Cup (1,3 inches wide) was bought by the Shanghai collector Liu Yquian and his wife Wang Wei for $ 38 million. This wine cup is on display in his private museum, which they founded in Shanghai in 2012.

Above: Wan Li period *kraak* porcelain dish with a bird decoration in the
central part. Date: 1580-1600, diam. 29.5 cm.
Right page: Chinese porcelain ribbed globular pot with depictions of
precious objects and peacock feathers in medallions, and
floral motifs top and bottom. Kangxi period, height 24.5 cm.

IMPALAS AND ZEBRAS
AT THE FRONT DOOR

When you go out of the door in the morning, don't be surprised

if you come face - to - face with a herd of impala or zebra.

This is the K'Shane estate, not far from Johannesburg in South

Africa. It is a large area on which a limited number of units have

been built in an architectural style that blends beautifully

with the natural surroundings.

The aim was to allow various African wildlife species to live in their

natural habitat without the buildings encroaching on their lives.

Since the residents did not want to discover that their carefully

planted gardens had served as dainty dishes for the animals,

natural fences can be found here and there.

One of the villas is colorfully furnished by

Brian Leib from Johannesburg.

**Left: Interior designer Brian Leib in the natural surroundings.
Right: African gazelles are all over the place at the K'Shane estate in South Africa.**

Right: The villa built in local materials, including timber, stone, and African thatch for the roof. The exterior wooden decking creates a natural transition between the living areas and the outdoor space. The garden is a paradise for the wild animals.

Below: The spacious living area on the left with the bar and spectacular wine atrium in the background. On the right of the photo, the dining room plus a second sitting area, and far right, the kitchen. In the background, the pool can be seen between the house and a second volume that is accessed over a suspended walkway.

The eco-friendly, game-orientated estate of K'Shane is but a short 67 kilometer commute from the Sandton suburb of Johannesburg. The development offers a unique lifestyle expression where residents coexist in harmony with the numerous wildlife species. Each of the 46 units occupies a 7,000–square meter stand on which the antelope species, including Blesbok, Blue Wildebeest, Impala, and Zebra, to name but few, roam freely.

Surrounded by the Magaliesberg mountains, the estate is situated on the banks of the Hartbeespoort Dam, a 195,000,000 cubic meter reservoir built along the Crocodile River in 1945. The name means "pass of the Hartbees" (an antelope in Afrikaans) and is frequented by weekend leisure seekers from both Pretoria and Johannesburg. Although specific requirements are set as to the appearance and architectural profiles of the exterior structures and landscaping, the interiors are naturally to the owner's personal preference.

The owners of this particular home took great care in the selection of their interior designer, they wanted someone who understood their energy and could interpret their emotional living into functional spaces. Flowing organized and clearly defined areas that are as aesthetically pleasing as they are functional were the main highlights of this brief, as was a subtle Balinese feel for the interior, but above all, the 1,200 m^2 house needed to be a home. They chose South African interior designer Brian Leib.

"The clients took a leap of blind faith," says Brian, having convinced them to accept a more colorful interior proposal than they had originally envisioned. In addition, the project, already in its third year was subjected to more Leib inspiration in the form of structural changes. The owners reluctantly conceded and were delighted with the outcome at conclusion.

Brian's interior style is transient, fusing together the organic and structural, the antique and the contemporary, a perfect blend of yin and yang. The exterior requirements prescribed a plethora of predominantly natural materials: timbers, stone and thatch (an African grass used for roofing) while walls had to be plastered in rough textured earthy tones. Timber decks constituted the external areas and indigenous landscaping is aimed at minimizing the overall aesthetic impact on the existing natural landscape.

The slate-clad columns of the main entrance give rise to the triple volume retreat-styled porte cochère. The entrance is set over a Koi pond and the Buddha statue adds to the Zen feel of the home's threshold. The large open plan living space is defined only by bulkhead ceiling detail. These multi-layered ceiling boxes house the home's lighting and sound equipment while breaking up the uniform pattern left by the shuttering of the cast slab. The main communal spaces, incorporating the kitchen, dining room, bar and living rooms, service the house's three en suite bedrooms. The off-set levels of these areas create interesting vantage points from which the views to the outside can be taken in.

The French oak flooring is a connective neutral base linking all the spaces. Bold fabrics in fuchsia, peppermint, lime, and blues accentuate the contemporary furniture.

Organic objects are interspersed as functional and aesthetic pieces. The floor is in part covered with a made-to-measure chocolate brown shaggy rug. The entire living area is enclosed by double volume bi-fold glass pane doors. Drapery in cool natural silk, cotton, and linen screens some of the over-abundant light provided by the sunny African skies. A twelve-seater dining room is central to the entertainment area. The kitchen and outdoor pool-side patio are only a few feet away.

The first-floor landing is stark, cool, and grey—a sombre departure from the vibrant colors used downstairs but well suited to introduce the sleeping quarters of the house. Travertine tiles modestly accessorized with a handwoven anemone-like sculpture lead you along the glass balustrade.

Top left: The floral inspired main suite has linen curtains, a silk rug and upholstery in a blue-green palette.

From the bedroom you have an uninterrupted view of the African landscape and you will wake to the sounds of the African bush.

Top right: The zen inspired entrance hall.

Below: Koi pond and the Buddha statue and one of the guest bathroom.

Bottom: The bathroom adjoining the master bedroom on the first floor of the main volume. The mirror reflects the splendid view that can be enjoyed from the adjoining deck. In the background, the outdoor stairs to the terrace at the top level.

Bottom right: The slate-clad columns of the main entrance.

Right: The zebra suite—one of the two guest sections—with artwork by Michelle Decker.

Next page:
The colorful living area at the pool side with, in the background, the dining table that seats 12 people.
The enormous wine cabinet, enclosed in green glass, is just visible on the right; there, wines are stored at the right temperature.

The roofing thatch is visible through the open trusses of the pitched roof. The upstairs area is divided into two sections. The main bedroom with en suite dressing rooms and the other wing serving as a guest area incorporating the zebra- and giraffe-themed suites.

From this area you can also access the fully-contained guest cottage with an additional two suites, kitchen, and living area. The floral inspired main suite has undisturbed views of the estate, a modern-day luxury where space is at a premium. For some, nothing could be more enjoyable than waking to the sounds of the African bush as golden sunshine comes streaming in.

"I like using soft color tones in bedrooms," says Leib, who believes that the tranquil environment is restful and relaxing, a place to unwind and take in the day's accomplishments. The strong taupe colors of the full-length linen drapes, carpet, and silk rug are complemented by a basic blue-green palette. "This space is both masculine and feminine," says Leib.

In the main bathroom, Leib uses mirrored surfaces to reflect the outdoors. The mosaic tiled wall panels of the vanities and shower enclosure are specifically designed from broken stone to mimic giraffe hide. The defining feature of the zebra suite is the painted canvas by South African artist Michelle Decker. A special commission by Leib to complement the black - and - white fabrics used throughout.

To complete the full functionality of this home, a suspended walkway links the main bedroom suite to an adjacent structure housing the office and gym, which is fully equipped with sauna, steam room, and Rasul spa. The lower portion of this building extends to the entertainment area of the poolside patio with the inclusion of a bar and games room.

"This lifestyle symbolizes something close to the African Dream," says Leib, "a sanctuary to work and play, and take in all of what this amazing country has to offer, but most of all one which you can call home."

INTERIORS
IN THE
COLORS
OF THE
DOGS

The dogs Salento and Sambelli who inspired the designers/architects Ludovica and Roberto Palomba in their choice of colors for the interior of their party/holiday home in the small Italian town of Sogliano Cavour in the South of Italy.

Right: The high old vaults in the former olive oil mill, which the Palombas transformed into a comfortable home that radiates tranquillity. The doors on the left open onto the central patio.

The dogs Salento and Sambelli—though they did not

realise it themselves—actually inspired designers/

architects Ludovica and Roberto Palomba in their

choice of colors for the interior of their holiday

home in the South of Italy.

In 2011 they purchased a former olive oil mill that

had been abandoned for over thirty years.

It is a remarkable old building with splendid vaults.

However, it required the insight of two talented

architects to look past the shambles and transform

the premises into a tranquil, comfortable dwelling.

Palomba Serafini Associati designed for:
Antolini, Bisazza, Boffi, Brix, Cappellini, Dornbracht, Driade, Elica, Elmar, Exteta, Fiam, Flaminia, Foscarini, KitchenAid, Kos, Laufen, Lema, Plank, Poltrona Frau, Rapsel, Redaelli, Salviati, Sawaya & Moroni, Samsung, Schiffini, Tubes, Valli&Valli, Viccarbe, When Objects Work, Zanotta, Zucchetti.

They live and work in Milan and purchased the old building in 2011, on the advice of a friend. They encountered an abandoned old olive oil mill that had been untouched for more than thirty years. On closer inspection, it turned out that the building had been constructed in three stages.
Roberto told something about it: "The first part is very old and was directly connected to the 17th-century Palazzo Mongio dell' Elefante close by. We believe it was in the palace gardens. The last part was built around 1800. In those days large quantities of olive oil was being produced in the region for use in oil lamps. You can still see many ancient olive trees dating from that period—the entire region

Below: The designers/architects Ludovica and Roberto Palomba. They work from their studio, Palomba Serafini Associati, which was founded in 1994. They have clients from the top of the international design world.
Left: The central court in their house in southern Italy. It is the hub of the interior and opens into the kitchen, the huge sitting room and open-air patio with a large hearth.

Next pages:
The large living room with the kitchen on the left. All the furniture and also the kitchen were designed by the Palombas themselves, for various furniture brands including, Zanotta, Kartell, Driade, Foscarini, and Exeta. The lamp above the table is a Flos creation.

was covered with them. Most of Europe used olive oil from this area for lighting. It was the Saudi Arabia of bygone days. The numerous fine old villas scattered around the countryside, often in deplorable condition, also date from that time. It was a prosperous region and Lecce, the capital, was a prosperous city. Interestingly, the people working in the local industry also took the products all round Europe. They worked here for six months and then went on their travels. In fact, few of them lived to a ripe old age. The days of riches ended when petroleum came on the scene." The focus of activities switched to tobacco growing.

Previous pages:
The master bedroom and en suite bathroom run parallel to the sitting room. The rooms are separated from the rest of the house with a door fitted with a large mirror on the sitting room side. The Palombas created the bathroom with fixtures of their own design, made by Zucchetti/Kos.
Next: the unusual, high vaulted space which is the bedroom.

These pages:
The open patio which provides light in the house. The whitewash reflects the sunlight; direct sunlight does not enter the house at all. The furniture was designed by the Palombas and is arranged in individual configurations in the interior. "They're all actors on the stage." The front of the house reveals nothing of the secret of the interior. Two small doors open into an oasis of peace and quiet. Old stairs lead to the bedrooms and terraces above.

"The old prosperous times are long gone. Today the area is geared to tourism and many people from northern Italy, and from abroad, are buying houses here. The region is very accessible from Milan or Rome. We invariably leave the studio at 6 pm and can be sitting here with friends by about 9 pm."
Roberto described what they encountered when they first looked round the mill. "For 'normal' people it was a dump. People said we were crazy. We're architects and can envisage how something can become. From the start Ludovica and I were enthusiastic about the space, the proportions and the potential. We'd renovated the premises in a matter of 5 months with a team of good craftsmen from the surroundings. The most important thing was to open up the structure and let the daylight flood into all the rooms. Fortunately we could open up the courtyard and now there's plenty of light throughout. In fact it's reflected light, as there's no direct sunlight anywhere in the house. That's particularly important in the summer—we can keep out the heat that way. We don't need air-conditioning; we just use the natural air flow."

That air flow is to some extent the result of the new floors. When they bought the property it had no flooring. Everything had first to be excavated to create proper floors with an air-circulation system underneath. The roofs were also caving in and had to be rebuilt—as did some of the walls, through which water was literally seeping. The walls were treated with mortar made from quicklime, which keeps the water out, kills harmful bacteria, and radiates beautiful, white-reflecting light.

When you stand in front of the house it's hard to picture the interior spaces. Two relatively small doors access the kitchen and the patio. From the kitchen, you step into the patio, which is still partly covered by the old vaults. In the summer this is the hub of the house. Behind the patio and kitchen, the sitting room extends along the entire width of the house. A door with a large mirror opens into the master bedroom and en suite bathroom. At one of the front doors a staircase takes you upstairs, passing a bedroom on the way. There are three bedrooms and bathrooms at the top of the stairs, and a door to the roof terraces, which are on different levels. Here, too, there is another separate bedroom area. In all, the house has seven bathrooms and lavatories.

Ludovica: "The house has been created for us to have a good time with our friends. One of our best friends lives in Palazzo Mongio dell' Elefante; every summer we spend a lot of time together. We always have many young friends staying with us. The house is so inviting. We renovated it with respect for the mood of the place. But we've also created something that's tailor made to our lifestyle." She had the following to say about the interior: "It's an interior where you walk around on bare feet. To shake off everything that's bad and start afresh. That's why the house is full of light, and at night we use candles to light it all up. We sit round the hearth. We also gave the furniture plenty of room— as if the pieces were actors on the stage. There's nothing against the walls. Those are simple things, but they're certainly important. Space and emptiness is important."

It has turned into a very comfortable house, in soft earth shades combined with the whitewashed surfaces. The furniture has been designed by the Palombas themselves and selected from the collections of manufacturers with whom they work.

Roberto wound up, saying: "We've created an interior with our own work, but it isn't a showroom. We aren't into "selfies." It's not about showing what we can do and have done. It's our personal taste. For Ludovica, the idea of emptiness is important. With a logical display, she has created a rich, spacious ambience which is reinforced by the architecture, the high ceilings and the white color. Our lives here are bound up with the earth. When the open fire is burning it seems as if there are no walls. We sit on the floor and the whole building seems to disappear. It's magic."

Above: The central patio seen from one of the three roof terraces. In the background, Palazzo Mongio dell' Elefante.
Right: The kitchen designed by the Palombas was made by Elmar Cucine.

Nexzt pages:
The living room with furniture designed by Ludovica and Roberto. The hearth on the floor is an unusual feature. On cold days, the owners and their guests gather there, sitting on the floor—like nomads on their ongoing journey.

MAXIME JACQUET

C H A N E L

m e e t s

M C Q U E E N

High fashion and art in one—that defines his design style. He rocketed to world renown when a

celebrated French fashion designer asked him to remodel his Los Angeles home. Several more

houses were to follow in Los Angeles, Miami, and Paris, as well as the interiors

of the fashion designer's yacht and private jet.

He has worked with David Guetta and other stars in Los Angeles. He designed a penthouse

in West Hollywood, which is a spectacular reflection of his approach to work.

Art—lots of art—is integrated in an interior that itself is a work of art. Maxime Jacquet's star

is rising at lightning speed. The designer hails from Belgium, but has since

called Los Angeles his home.

The penthouse that Maxime Jacquet designed, is located in the Sunset Vine Tower in West Hollywood, Los Angeles. When he first saw the apartment it was practically empty, a cold space without personality. The internal arrangement was basic, the colors off-white. The space was intended to have the ambience of an elegant loft—a Los Angeles loft, less industrial than one in New York.

"When I came here the first time, I felt like a child in a sweet shop. The rooms were spacious, with large windows. I knew right away that I could create something here that would blow everyone away. As it was, the apartment was devoid of character. Now it has a great deal of character, because, starting from nothing, I have been able to add everything. I particularly wanted dark walls and color, lots of color. People told me to use a minimum of furniture, to leave the view unspoilt. I was convinced that in the end you get used to the view, whereas the interior you live in is something that affects you directly—the art, the fabrics, textures, objects are constantly changing and they speak to you," to use Maxime's own words.

"For me, color is very important. I love dark colors because they give you a feeling of security. Not black, but all the variations on warm, dark shades. In my work an important first step is to determine the colour and texture of the walls. The second step is the art. An interior without art is like a person without personality.

I couldn't possibly create something without art. You must express who you are as a person, and art plays an important part in that. That's why one of the chief aspects of an interior project is the art you select together with your clients. You must take time to discover what they like."

This apartment, with views over the whole of Los Angeles, from the hills to the sea, is living proof of his views on art. The space comprises a large central area, which also houses the kitchen with cooking island. Flanking the living room there are two bedrooms with en suite bathrooms. Artworks are scattered throughout the apartment. Hermès Birkin and Louis Vuitton suitcases have been placed, seemingly carelessly and liberally, as objects in the interior. He clearly has a preference for everything vintage. Maxime: "I'm a real collector. I buy everything that appeals to me and I don't look at the price. Art and attractive things come at a price, but it's all about what those objects mean to you. It seems full here, but if I see something beautiful I buy it. There's always room for beauty."

Left: The master suite with a bed from the Maxime Jaquet collection.
Right: The guest bedroom with fabrics by Missoni; the lamp with mother-of-pearl discs is by Verner. The Ray Ban illustration is by Sebastian Onufszak.

Next pages:
The master suite with the stunning view over Los Angeles towards the ocean. The big green apple is a sculpture sourced from Bull & Stein, the bedding is by Fendi and the natural kraft paper console came from Molo. The white ball chair is by Eero Aarnio and the white floor lamp beside it is by Arne Jacobsen for Louis Poulsen Lighting. Takashi Murukami designed the travel trunk for Louis Vuitton. The large ceiling mobile is by Alexander Calder.

His star has risen rapidly. He was born in Belgium in 1992 and, when he was a child, travelled the world with his parents. He studied art and history in the Belgian city of Leuven. At that stage he was a restorer of art objects. A website with photos of his own interior was reason enough for a French fashion tycoon to commission him to design the interior of one of his homes in the city where Jaquet longed to live: Los Angeles. Those assignments formed the foundations for his fame. He was just 19 years old.
"I'd often been to LA and knew it was where I wanted to live. When the request came in I said 'yes' right away. I'd no idea how to tackle it, hardly spoke the language, but I wasn't apprehensive because I knew I could design something special to reflect his personality. That's just what I did and in that same year I did a couple more projects for the same client, including a yacht and a private jet."

Maxime's basic principle is clear: "I follow my passion. Important sources of inspiration are fashion and the street scene. I do things stemming from my own creative mood. I don't care what other people have to say. I'm not scared of doing things people have never seen before. After that first big job, everything snowballed and it never stopped! In recent years I've been able to set up a team to put my ideas into effect."

And he went on: "The guiding principle is always to create a liveable, attractive and contemporary interior. In my mind interiors are not timeless. Some things you keep your entire life because you like them, not because they're timeless. Timelessness isn't a big deal for me. I design things to be enjoyed now. I always tell my clients that their taste changes, as does their lifestyle. And that also changes the interaction with the interior. I tend to be someone who looks at what's happening in the street and in fashion. They influence the way I see design—it's the way I live."

"ROCK & ROLL QUEEN"
YOU ARE THE SUN
YOU ARE THE ONLY ONE
MY HEART IS BLUE
MY HEART IS BLUE FOR YOU
E MY, BE MY, BE MY LITTLE
ROCK AND ROLL QUEEN
E MY, BE MY, BE MY LITTLE
ROCK AND ROLL QUEEN
YOU ARE THE SUN
U ARE THE ONLY ONE
YOU ARE SO COOL
U ARE SO
ROCK AND ROLL
E MY, BE MY LITTLE
CK AND ROLL QUEEN
MY, BE MY LITTLE
ROCK AND ROLL QUEEN
BE MY, BE MY LITTLE ROCK AND ROLL QUEEN
BE MY, BE MY LITTLE ROCK AND ROLL QUEEN
YOU ARE THE SUN
YOU ARE THE ONLY ONE
YOU ARE SO COOL
IT'S ALL SO ROCK AND ROLL

THE BEYLERIANS IN THE WOODS

The house is set in the wooded surroundings of Kent, a small town in Connecticut about two hours' drive from

Manhattan. It rises up like a group of interlocking building volumes at the end of a driveway, where a substantial

herd of deer usually awaits the caller. It is the home of Louise and George Beylerian, situated on a hillside with

panoramic views of the surrounding gardens and woods beyond.

That in itself is a charming sight, but the interior is what is really exceptional: a medley of items of major design

furniture and objects from recent decades, a large array of modern art and several other special collections.

Hardly surprising, since George Beylerian played a pivotal role in bringing Italian design to the American market.

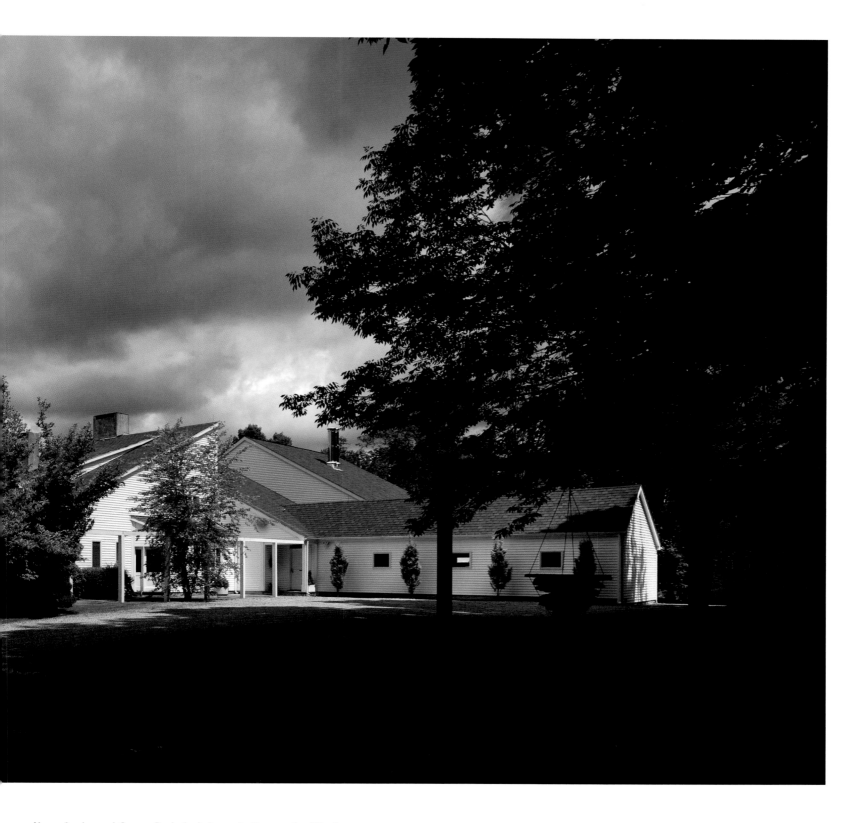

Above: Louise and George Beylerian's house in the woods of Kent,
Connecticut. This is the front elevation. At the back, a large volume
was recently added and the outline of the roof is just visible here.
They commute from their house in the woods every week to New
York City where George runs his Material ConneXion. The hanging
artwork in the garden is by Gregory Beylerian: prayers have been
wedged into the piles of suspended stones.

George Beylerian hates doing nothing. That, at least, is clear. He divides his time between his work in Manhattan and his house in the country. But he doesn't sit still, even when he's in Kent—he has an office there where he sits until the early hours, checking through the most important magazines, newspapers, and, in particular, catalogues of international art auctions.
Louise and George's home was built in 1983 by an English architect who clearly liked the traditional country-house style. When the couple acquired it in 1987, it did not look the way it does today.

George: "In the beginning we used it as a weekend house. It only became our permanent home in 2006, when we left our place in Manhattan. Since then we have divided our time between weekends here and three days of work in the city, where we have an apartment. When we moved permanently we realized we needed an extension. In 2008 we completed an addition that has almost doubled the floor area to 800 square meters. The form of the extension was largely our own idea. We were assisted by our friend, the architect David Ling, who provided valuable input. For instance, he was the one who advised us to concentrate the windows in the large living area in one corner, leaving more wall space to hang art."

The original house can best be described as a number of shapes inspired by seemingly interlaced local sheds. The complex is built on a hillside and follows the contours of the slope. The different levels that now occur inside mean that there is more space indoors that would appear from the outside.
And yet there is still not enough room for all the design objects and artworks. That would be expecting too much! Even after the substantial extension, much of the collection has to be kept in special climate-controlled storage space. The addition comprised a large rectangular volume at the back of the house. Part of it, under the sloping roof, is open to the ridge, and a mezzanine floor has been built to house, in succession, the master bedroom, bathroom, and Louise's study.

The spacious ground floor contains an open plan sitting room with various seating areas around the central fireplace. The windows are placed to leave maximum wall space for showing artworks. A series of window-elements is concentrated in the corner where an outdoor balcony has been set against the façade like a drawbridge. The house also has three guestrooms plus a small additional bedroom, a dining room, an art gallery, media room, and George's office. The patio sat the back overlook the downhill sloping grounds and gardens, the swimming pool in natural hues, a large, grassy meadow, and the woods.

An interesting aspect of the collection is that every piece of furniture, every artwork and every item of fabric tells a story. In fact, you will find the entire history of furniture design of recent decades here. Walking through the house, George keeps going off at a tangent: every single important name in furniture design crops up. He talks about his experiences with Jo Colombo and Verner Panton, Philip Starck and Ingo Maurer.
Many of the designers have become their friends. The collection not only includes design furniture, on the contrary, there is a great deal of modern

Top left: The stairs to the gallery with, in the foreground, a work by Patrick Gaughan. The chair behind that is by Vitra.
Right: The hallway beyond the main entrance of the house with part of the collection of boxes in the cabinet left, and an antique Biedermeier sofa.

Middle row: The Beylerians' house seen from poolside, and beside that, the extension with outdoor balcony set, floating like a drawbridge against the sitting area.

Below left: Looking from the gallery on the lower floor containing a lamp by Stefan Lindfors. Against the back wall, an electronic art piece by Ara Hovsepyan.
The chair in between is by Gaetano Pesce. On the table, Neal Small's Air Museum. The large armchair is by Kenneth Cobonpue and the sofa in the foreground is a creation of Gaetano Pesce's. On the wall right, *Conflict* by Wey-Jeng Hwang. On the right the cabinet containing part of George Beylerian's miniature chair collection.

A composition with an armchair by Kenneth Cobonpue, an African figure, and artwork by Wey-Jeng Hwang.

art, as well as an important collection of Coptic textiles, miniature chairs and decorative boxes.

"The collection has come about over the years. The furniture dates from the days when I was in the chair business. Little by little, we purchased and collected the rest in the time-honored way. Our art also determines the interior design of our house: entirely non referential. That's what Louise and I like. Not a style or a period, but an eclectic totality—a real "house-house.""

They've been married for 45 years. Both were born in Egypt, of Armenian descent. When the various family businesses in Egypt were nationalized, they moved to America at the end of the '50s.

George graduated in marketing and business studies with distinction from the New York University, after which he threw himself into interior design. As a champion of modern Italian design, he began spreading the gospel early on from his store, Scarabaeus, which he opened in 1964. It was the first high-end concept store in the heart of Manhattan and, as

a world premiere, soon followed by his introduction of Kartell plastic furniture, introducing color to the American interior with that furniture manufacturer: primrose colors became a major trend.

He then entered the contract market, bombarding it with his Contract Collection: design products by prestigious designers. It appealed to leading players in that market and Steelcase made Beylerian an offer he couldn't refuse. His involvement was to set off a veritable upgrading of the Steelcase image and business.

As Vice President and Creative Director, he altered the company's course in keeping with his own, unique approach and perspective. He organized a number of trail-blazing exhibitions to elevate Steelcase's identity to a higher plane. They included *Life, Work, Tools* featuring the tools of artists, performers and innovative entrepreneurs, and *Mondo Materialis* in which he asked 150 of the world's top architects and designers for their ideas on the materials of the future. It led to an exhibition in New York's Guggenheim Museum.

Above: Triptych painting by Caroline McNairn.

Row of chairs from left to right: Gaetano Pesce armchair for Cassina, Gaetano Pesce chair for Cassina, Marcel Wanders knotted chair, chrome chair by Shiro Kuramata, Bentwood armchair with cork striped covering for Gebruder Thonet, Frank Lloyd Wright armchair for Cassina, Bambi armchair by Borek Cipek.

Right: Seats by Gaetano Pesce.

such, admired by many, including Susan Grant Lewin (today an esteemed colleague at OBJEKT©International) who was the first to write about it. The focus at Scarabaeus was on modern, cutting-edge products in which the distinction between art and design was blurred. Pop Art was hung alongside Mexican handwork, and Art Nouveau objects rubbed shoulders with the creative products of emergent Italian designers. There was no other place in America combining such a range of cultures. And George's strong personal conviction was the basis for its success.

Beylerian's "Something Else" collection altered the interiors landscape of the United States instantly. The shop-in-shop formula turned it into a major high-end accessories collection. It was nothing less than a revolution in modern design retailing. The next milestone was his Casa Idea, a store-in-store at Bloomingdales. According to Beylerian it was

George Beylerian continued to be consumed by the theme of materials for the future, which ultimately resulted in his initiative for Material ConneXion—in his opinion, the missing link between the world of high-tech materials and that of design professionals.

George knows them all: the influential designers of the last fifty years. He still has close friendships with many of them and can recount his adventures with creative celebrities for hours on end.

"The first Italian designers were usually out-of-work architects. They laid the foundations for what is now called Italian design," as George Beylerian explained.

They inspired him recently to create *Design Memorabilia*, a collection of iconic designs by Italians masters. The first collection is called *De Gustibus* which loosely translates from the Latin to: About taste. This will be presented at Expo Milano 2015.

Above: The sitting room in the new extension which houses part of the collection of art and furniture objects. On the wall left, a triptych by Caroline McNairn, chairs by Marcel Wanders, also the Shiro Kuramata chair, chairs by Thonet and Frank Lloyd Wright, and Borek Sipek's Bambi chair. Beside the sofa, an America Craft chair. Above the fireplace, a fluorescent object by Craig Kauffman. In the space on the right above the chairs, a work by Muir Beveridge. On the wall right, a self portrait by Gaetano Pesce, a Paul Sarkisian diptych and a work by Arman entitled *Embedded Garbage*.
Right: The bathroom between the master bedroom and Louise's study on the first floor.
Far right: The master bedroom with, right, an artwork by Michelangelo Pistoletto and above a sofa by De Pas, D'Urbino and Lomazzi. The cupboards against the back wall are from Ikea.

The living room in the Beylerian house with two English armchairs and, on the back wall, a self-portrait by Gaetano Pesce. The light fixture beside the fireplace is Paul Sasso's *Ou La La*.
Above the table: The Gino Sarfatti chandelier by Flos. The chairs around the table and the dish were designed by Gaetano Pesce.

PHILIP JOHNSON'S GLASS HOUSE

For over 75 years Philip Johnson (1906-2005) was a leading figure in American architecture.

Initially he worked as a curator at the MoMA (Museum of Modern Art) in New York and went

on to design an awesome series of large and small edifices including the AT&T Building (now

Sony Plaza) in New York and the Crystal Cathedral in Garden Grove, California.

During his lifetime, his most important building was rarely seen, apart from in photos. It is the

Glass House (1949) in New Canaan, Connecticut, where he lived for 50 years.

Previous pages
**Left: A corner of the bedroom in the Glass House.
Minimalism *avant la lettre*, with furniture designed
by Mies van der Rohe.**

These pages
**Above: The Glass House which belonged to the architect
Philip Johnson in New Canaan, in Connecticut. The area teems
with houses built by Johnson and his contemporary, Marcel
Breuer.**

Next pages:
**The large open space in the Glass House harmonizing with
the natural surroundings.**

The Glass House is an icon of architecture on account of the modernist transparency in which it abounds.
With four sheet glass walls and a simple steel frame, it merges seamlessly into its breathtaking setting
of charming grassy slopes, sturdy old trees and a 19th-century stone wall. In this house, Johnson felt at
one with nature.

It was also where he received guests, including Frank Lloyd Wright, the architect who was 40 years his elder.
It was rumored that, when visiting the Glass House for the first time, Wright asked, "Philip, am I inside or out?
Do I take my hat off or leave it on?"

If one wishes to appreciate Johnson's importance for American architecture, it is useful to conceptualize the
glass skyscrapers that characterized present-day cities. In the 1930s New York was experiencing a craze for
Art Deco, which was very far removed from the taut structures designed by Mies van der Rohe, Walter Gropius
or Le Corbusier. 1932 was the year in which New York hailed its first skyscrapers: the Chrysler and the Empire
State Buildings. It was also the year in which Philip Johnson curated the legendary MoMA *International Style*
exhibition. The title of the exhibition refers to the book Johnson co-authored with Henry-Russell Hitchcock, the
leading American architectural historian of his day. The much-debated, visionary book immediately catapulted
Johnson to prominence as one of the foremost figures in American architecture. And he continued to fulfill that
role until his death in 2005.

However, in 1932 Johnson was not yet an architect, only resuming his studies in the 1940s after his successes at the MoMA. He graduated in 1943 from Harvard University, leaving his comfortable position at the MoMA to try his hand as an architect. Whereas, at the museum he had been surrounded by people of a like mind (Professor Barr shared his view of architecture as art), he encountered an entirely different mentality at Harvard. Lectures were given by Walter Gropius who had founded the Bauhaus in Weimar. Philip Johnson had visited it in the 1920s and was not particularly friendly with Gropius. He accused him of considering the functional aspect more important than the artistic. The following is a notorious quote from that time: "I would rather sleep all night in Chartres Cathedral and walk down the street to the john than spend the night in a Harvard house with back-to-back plumbing."

But his admiration was all the greater for the artistic Ludwig Mies van der Rohe, in whose work architectural grandeur always transcended comfort. Mies's influence is particularly apparent in Johnson's early work.
The house he built for himself in 1942 in Cambridge, Massachusetts, is completely based on the Miesian Court Houses—a new concept for urban living. With it, Johnson created a *loft-avant-la-lettre* with one wall in glass overlooking a small walled garden. Ash Street, as it would later be called, was the precursor of the Glass House, which is a distinctive mixture of pure international style and Johnson's personal taste. It is no mere architectural

Top right: The bedroom in the house of architect Philip Johnson, enclosed entirely in glass. The cupboard serves as a division between that room and the living space.
Below: The large open living area with furniture designed by Mies van der Rohe. The painting, *Burial of Phocion* (1648-1649), is attributed to Nicolas Poussin. The sculpture Two *Circus Women* is by Elie Nadelman and dates from 1930.

This page top left: The first site-specific work by Donald Judd (1971). Judd could be termed the figurehead of Minimalism. In exchange for a work by Frank Stella, he created a taut concrete circle in a response to the transparency of the Glass House. This was the first time in history that artistic use was made of building materials. Judd's intention was to create a bridge between sculpture and architecture.
Top right: The square, closed form as a counterpoint to the transparency of the Glass House.
Below left: The pool in a composition of straight line and circle; the interior of the Library/Study and looking upwards in the light well. The entrance to the bathroom is situated inside the cylinder located in the interior. On the other side of the volume there is a fireplace.

concept, but was to serve as a home. It is interesting, not because of the blend of Miesian and classical architectural principles, but particularly on account of the way the design engages with the natural surroundings. "Trees are the basic building block on the place," was Johnson's motto.

Despite the patently obvious influences of Mies van der Rohe, Johnson did not consider himself to be Miesian. Which is strange, when you realize that much of the furniture in the house was designed by Mies. However, all becomes clear when you discover that Mies was disappointed with the Glass House. Not on account of the similarities, but actually the dramatic differences. To start with, the symmetrical façades and the brick floor, which he did not care for. He really disliked the cylindrical central core which housed a fireplace and a bathroom. Mies even refused to spend the night there, which in turn upset Johnson. Still, it did not put Johnson off and one of his most telling adages was: "The day of ideology is thankfully over. There are no rules, only facts. There is no order, only preference, there are no imperatives, only choice or taste."

He evidently continued to stand by his assertion, as can be seen from the structures dotted around the estate. Moreover, the estate is reminiscent of a diary, if only because Johnson continued to add buildings

The Library/Studio which Philip Johnson built around 1980. It is shaped like a cube with a cylindrical volume in the corner serving as a lightwell. In the background, the red Gate House beside the official entrance to the estate.

with clockwork regularity over fifty years. First there was the Pavilion. It stands beside a lake and was designed to be admired from the main building higher up the slope. Only when seen from closer by it is clear that the fanciful structure is quite small. It is a playful reference to the clever architectural interventions of cathedral builders in olden days who dramatized effects and made them more distorted using scale and perspective.
Francesco Borromini, the architect of the Baroque church of San Carlo alle Quattro Fontane in Rome, was a particular favorite of Johnson's.

The Painting Gallery and the Sculpture Gallery followed in 1965 and 1970, almost twenty years after the principal building.
The Sculpture Gallery stands on a slope and has pitched glass roofs. The irregular, stepped construction makes for unexpected impressions and calls forth an unusual spatial experience.

Later on, Johnson would elaborate further on the geometrical distortions he used here. The building is a splendid framework for the superlative artworks that Johnson collected with his life partner, David Whitney. The works, together with the gallery in which they are displayed, constitute a dramatic lesson in Modernism. There is work by Elie Nadelman, Andy Warhol, Bruce Nauman, Frank Stella, and even a Nicolas Poussin from 1648-49. However, the most important artwork is in the garden. It is a site-specific work by Donald Judd (1971). Judd could be termed the figurehead of Minimalism. Here, in exchange for a large object by Frank Stella, he created a taut concrete circle in a response to the transparency of the Glass House.

Ten years after the Sculpture Gallery, Johnson built himself a Library/Study. A remarkable structure in which he once more examined light, space, and scale. The property is on a slope which means that the ground plan is rectangular, but the building itself is cube-shaped. The pure geometrical lines are interrupted by a cylindrical volume in the corner which serves as a light well. Daylight pouring into the library gives it an almost spiritual character. His last work, the red Gate House, also challenges set geometrical patterns—this time Johnson has gone quite far.
Although the building is intended as a visitors' center, it has a visually disorientating effect. It is a silent witness to Johnson's growing fascination with spatial experiments and sensational effects.
Today the Glass House can be visited as a museum. Johnson had painstakingly prepared the transference of the house to the National Trust for Historic Preservation. However, during restoration of the site, he realized he was becoming increasingly fond of ruins. For instance, he praised the decay of the New York State Pavilion which he built for the 1964-65 World's Fair:
"There ought to be a university course in the pleasure of ruins", was his conclusion.

Above: The interior of the red Gate House—a silent witness to Johnson's growing fascination with spatial experiments and sensational effects.
Below: The Painting Gallery is built underground into a mound topped by 'circles, The artworks depicted here, from left to right: Frank Stella's *Konskie III*, 1971, *Tetuan II*, 1964, Averroes, 1960, *Darabjerd I*, 1967, *Lanckorona II*, 1971.
Right: The bronze tree trunk lying on a base, also in bronze, links the Sculpture and Painting Galleries (entrance in background). It is a work by Julian Schabel.

Next pages
The Sculpture Gallery sits on a slope and has pitched glass roofs. It is a spectacular architectural structure housing equally spectacular art. Works include: Frank Stella, *Raft of Medusa, Part I*, 1990, Robert Morris, *Untitled*, 1965-70, Andrew Lord, *27 Pieces, Modelling, Silver and Bismuth*, 1991-92, and John Chamberlain, *H.A.W.K.*, 1959.

SHAO FAN
BEYOND BEAUTY

He is world renowned for his deconstructions of

Chinese furniture: modern, three-dimensional art

based on traditional Chinese culture.

"What is really transcendent is beauty. Beauty is more

than religion, politics, even more than culture."

Shao Fan lives and works with his wife Anna Liu Li in

a complex he designed himself north of the Chinese

capital Beijing. With his work, he has become an icon

symbolizing China's modern transformation.

An 'incurable classicist' whose work is included

in the permanent collections of important

museums worldwide.

Left: An iconic object created by the artist Shao Fan: *Project No. I* of 2004, a deconstruction of a traditional Chinese furniture item made in elm wood and acrylic glass.
Right: Shao Fan in the doorway to his house-cum-studio in Shunyi district north of the Chinese capital Beijing.

"Contemporary courtyard living" is the way the artist Shao Fan describes his studio-cum-home in Shunyi district north of Beijing. It is an area where international schools display signs inviting the brightest and the best to enroll. A few years ago he bought a large plot of land there for which he conceived a unique architectural plan: a cutting-edge design uniting a modern Western lifestyle and the traditional approach to living space. A modern version of a *hutong* (collection of urban courtyard residences), but in the countryside.

He proceeded to realize his plans, but with the intention to share the complex with five friends – also artists. It is an oasis of peace and quiet, where the grey-blue stone in which it is built acquires an extra dimension thanks to the surrounding greenery.

His own studio and home consists of a series of rectangular spaces, one following on from the other. They

are separated by courtyards. In one of the courtyards Shao Fan has a rare plum tree. He has used it as a reference to the fact this species frequently occurs in Chinese poetry and paintings. His courtyard gardens have received many an accolade from connoisseurs.

This is where he lives with his wife Anna Liu Li, who is also an artist. Here he makes his deconstructions of traditional Chinese furniture, his paintings and other objects. He comes across as retiring, but he has definite ideas about his art. He describes himself as one of the first Chinese artists to explore the boundaries between visual art and design.
He was born in 1964, into a renowned Beijing artist family. Shao Fan excelled in art, especially in painting. He received his first painting instruction during the Cultural Revolution, from parents who were university art

Previous pages
Left: A 2-meter long *Ming Spine,* 2006, made in tieli wood, and a Ming chair in catalpa and elm.
Right: *Ming Beard,* 2006, in red sandalwood, 43 x 152 x 12 cm.

These pages:
The entrance and reception area in Shao Fan's studio complex, including two polished steel Ming chairs. He also made the large painting.

professors assigned to paint Mao Zedong propaganda. His sister Shao Fei is also a well-known Chinese artist. He graduated from the Beijing Arts and Crafts College in 1984 and began exploring three-dimensional art. His attraction to design, combined with a profound interest in Chinese culture, compelled him to research woodcarvings and ceramics, and led to his own signature style.

Shao began to paint professionally in 1989, but his passion remained rooted in three-dimensional art, which eventually led to the creation of objects that integrate both art and design.

In the beginning, his paintings were very much under the influence of Western modern art, just like most Chinese artists who were trained in Chinese art schools. When he turned thirty, something changed.

Above: A Buddha dating from the Qing dynasty, China's last Imperial dynasty, lasting from 1644 to 1912.
Beside that: An antique Tibetan chest, upholstered in sheepskin. In front, a Tibetan tiger rug.

Right: Five Leg Table 2011, in red sandalwood, 88.5 x 100 x 30 cm.

A small seed that was planted long ago in Shao Fan's mind started to grow. His artwork went back to the traditional Chinese art, but with a contemporary twist. The seed was sown by his grandma, who educated Shao when he was very small.

His parents were often away travelling and to some extent he was brought up by his grandmother, who was an educated lady from an aristocratic family (Qi Ren) of the Qing dynasty. She taught him what it is like to live like an aristocrat, what to eat, what to wear and how to talk, explained him the beauty of old things.

This impression became more obvious when he was a little older. "Back then, the country was not rich like it is now: the objects we used in everyday life were ugly compared to the antiques." So his appreciation for traditional forms became more deeply rooted.

Years later Shao Fan started to acquire antiques, played around with them and learned how to make and break them. He now believes there is a balance between the artistic design of a piece of furniture and the artisanship of building it. "In the past two hundred years, there has been less and less attention for the techniques of how to build things," Shao said. "To call someone an artisan was often not perceived as a compliment, while it actually is."

Perhaps that is the main secret of Shao's success in whichever field he has touched. Just when you thought he was a great oil painter, a furniture designer, a practical architect, he became a garden designer—illustrated by the fact that his creation, called *This is Not a Chinese Garden*, won a gold medal at the

Above: One of the central courtyards with entrance to the garden with the pagoda.
Right: The antique pagoda in all its splendor.
Shao Fan has designed his own courtyards and gardens. He even participated as a garden designer in the most important garden festival in the world: the RHS Chelsea Flower Show in London, England. His creation *This is Not a Chinese Garden*, won a gold medal in the 2008 show.

Next pages:
Shao Fan in his salon, the central space between his studios and reception areas.

RHS Chelsea Flower Show in 2008. This garden was intended to look like a Chinese archaeological site. "To integrate Western and Eastern culture is a tricky thing, these two don't really interface. (Perhaps it is a good thing.) What makes us happy is to come back to where we all started, at least the past two thousand years of Chinese history is a kind of repetition of going around and coming back."
When you enter his studio through the large black doors you arrive in a large reception area in predominantly shades of grey, black, and white. High windows and doors overlook two small patios and one large one. A large painting by Shao Fan hangs on the wall, flanked by polished steel Ming chairs. Antique Chinese furniture is arranged along the walls. Other than that, the space is empty and serene.
His work spaces are located on the other side of the large patio and comprise a sitting room with two large studios beyond. Here again, tranquillity prevails, and the antique and modern artworks come to life.
Everything tells its own story, like the sober, classic red seat contrasting with the lavish white fur, or the serene sandalwood Ming Beard, 2006. It measures one-and-a-half meters and balances delicately on its wooden pedestal. In this space there is also a Qing dynasty Buddha from Jiangxi province which Anne Liu Li found during an antiques hunt. A passage leads from the central patio to another patio containing an antique pagoda, and on to the artists' house. It is a world of peace in surroundings where speed and energy are the magic words, with Beijing as the epicenter.

In his painting and

sculpture Shao Fan

deftly blends East

and West with

the contemporary and

the traditional.

His work seeks a balance

among form, function,

elegance, and

the serenity of nature.

- The New York Times -

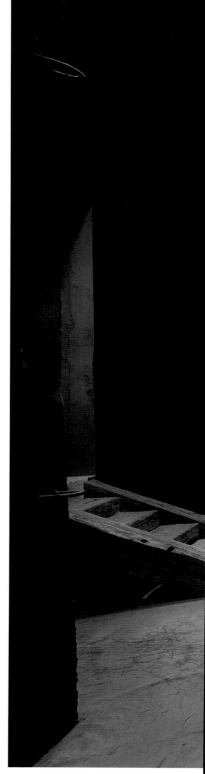

Above: May and Axel Vervoordt with their two sons, Dickie and Boris.
Right: Serenity achieved in the contrast of the wooden, partially lacquered Lohan figure dating from the 13th century and its bleak setting between the dark walls of Het Kanaal's industrial premises. The sculpture represents a monk at the highest level of meditation.

Next pages:
The Black Room at Het Kanaal complex emanates the tranquillity of simplicity. Here, a large sofa, a sturdy table in front of it, and several chairs on either side form the décor for the artworks on the walls. Left, a large photo by Frank Thiel; above the sofa a work by Hermann Goepfert; and right, works by Riccardo di Marchi.

AXEL VERVOORDT'S MAGIC

Axel Vervoordt's name is known throughout the world. His fame as an art and antiques dealer and consummate collector

beggars description. He possesses the talent to combine eclectic items—such as old and new, antiques and modern art—

to form a harmonious whole and create a palette of simplicity. Time and again, his achievements and vision can count on

tremendous enthusiasm. One of the many memorable occasions being *Artempo: Where Time Becomes Art*,

the impactive exhibition in Palazzo Fortuny in Venice in 2007 which was part of the Biennial of Contemporary Art.

He has a great fondness for *Wabi-Sabi*, Japanese aesthetic of the beauty of imperfection.

Above: The Karnak room in its former glory with several Dvaravati statues (7th and 8th centuries) from Northern Thailand.

Right: A work by Anish Kapoor, *At the Edge of the World*. It dates from 1998 and was installed in a special room at Het Kanaal complex in June 2000. It completed a veritable pilgrimage before landing in this almost perfect exhibition space. The dome has a diameter of 8 meters and a height of 5 meters. The Anish Kapoor will be the centre of a new Vervoordt city project at the Kanaal.

The foundations for the Vervoordt empire were laid in Antwerp, Belgium in a narrow alley called Vlaekensgang. That was where Axel Vervoordt started out as an antique dealer working from his home. His purchase of the Castle of 's-Gravenwezel in 1984 was a bold move. It is a 13th-century castle with double ramparts and set in a park. He went to live there with his family and his creative genius blossomed in those surroundings. At the castle he has received and entertained countless celebrities, especially from the cultural scene. In 1999 he purchased Het Kanaal site in Wijnegem which, prior to that, had housed one of Europe's largest malt-processing plants. Originally he had intended to use the industrial building as a warehouse for antiques he was unable to display at the castle, but it rapidly became a Vervoordt statement in its own right. The family then came up with an ambitious plan: a complex entitled Kanaal. A City in the Country.

Axel Vervoordt explained: "The essence of this 'city' is to revive an old industrial location. I really love this kind of architecture because it's genuine. We are living in times of recycling; there's no room to keep on making new things and throwing old things away. We called in good, contemporary architects to help revive the old industrial premises. The heart of the complex is Anish Kapoor's *At the Edge of the World* from 1998. The installation is synonymous with the fullness of emptiness. It gives body to the voice. It demonstrates that everything is derived from emptiness. That is the new spiritual blood and it's going to breathe life into the new city. It will be a greatly powerful, human, and sensitive place where people from all walks of life can meet. Status and money play no part in the selection—we want to appeal to people who are interested in art, music, and a harmonious lifestyle to attract lots of artists."

OBJEKT©International had a few questions for Axel Vervoordt.
Who are your favorite artists and designers?
"Artists and designers are two entirely different categories for me. Art is what fascinates me most: both very old, universal art that emanates tranquillity and intelligence, as well as the many different facets of modern art. I like things made by shepherds high in the mountains with tremendous perception and highly minimalist in form: anonymous art that acquires perfection as time passes and in which time itself is the artist. That was the focus of Artempo; I've written several books on the subject. It's a source of inspiration for me. But artists like Lucio Fontana, Anish Kapoor, Jef Verheyen, and Kazuo Shiraga are also an inspiration: the concept of emptiness from which new harmony is sought between mankind and nature in art. The influence of the East and Eastern Philosophy—I began collecting from that perspective. You also see the same inspirations and guiding principles in my work. I can talk about it indefinitely!"

Do you have favorite cities?
"I really love the outdoor life: I live in the country. But it's important to visit inspiring cities. I often go to New York for exhibitions and for the energy the city radiates. I think Venice is a fantastic city because there are no cars and I encounter lots of writers and artists there. The combination of the old, time-worn palazzos and contemporary art is at its best there. Osaka, Japan. is an interesting, modern city with many artists, but I prefer to meet the artists living somewhere isolated high in the mountains.

Where do you prefer to live and work: Europe, America or Asia?
"Europe. But for me the most important thing is that the people I work with interest me; people who are intelligent and with whom you can have a good conversation. Many of the people I work with have become friends. When I design someone's home, it's certainly not about outward appearances. It's much deeper

In which period would you like to have been born and have lived?
"Most definitely the present. I'm a person who lives for the day: every moment is important, from a walk in the park in the morning to breakfast, and from the moment I start work until dinner beside the fire. I try to make the best of every moment in harmony with the sum total. That's luxury for me: the feeling of being in harmony with circumstances."

What, in your view, is essential in a home?
"We're lucky enough to live in a very old castle in which the influences of many different periods are always present. For me, it's important that I can sit in the place that matches my mood at that moment. My study is furnished in classic English style. I can concentrate there. The library has a different ambience: there I can read, and sometimes I go and sit in my almost empty Wabi room to study something or to talk to special people."

than that; I try to approach it with philosophy and profundity that isn't specific to a particular region."

Do you have favorite hotels and what conditions must they meet?
"First and foremost, I stays hotels generally when I'm travelling for business. Then I prefer a modern, efficient, and not over-large hotel. I detest all those hotels in pseudo-French style and with the pretence of luxury. For me, luxury is something genuine. I like hotels where interesting people stay, like Robert de Niro's Greenwich Hotel in New York. It's not particularly big and it's congenial. Another favorite is Miya Masou in the mountains north of the Japanese city of Kyoto in a 16th century monastery. Other than that, it's a treat to be at home: to enjoy the castle and the gardens. The feeling of being at home is real luxury, in my view."

Left: Storerooms and exhibition rooms in Het Kanaal have been designed as small works of art. Here a cabinet of curiosities in the complex.

Above
One of the large areas at Het Kanaal, by Axel Vervoordt used for interior display.

Artempo: Where Time Becomes Art in Het Kanaal
a living memory of the compelling exhibition in
Venice's Palazzo Fortuny in 2007 as part of the
Biennial of Contemporary Art. It was an exhibition that positively amazed the art world and was
based on the idea that time is the greatest artist
of all. The spectacular event occupied all the imposing palazzos' rooms and addressed the
relationships between art, time, and the power
that a presentation can emanate.

A MASTERPIECE BY
THIERRY W. DESPONT
ON HARBOUR ISLAND

He is one of the foremost interior architects of recent decades, of his day
in fact. He is a master at fusing classical and modern into a
timeless totality. And that is also true for his architecture.
Thierry W. Despont, who hails originally from France and has his office in
New York, has enriched the world with his striking creations.
In his design for a holiday retreat on the Bahamas, nature and
architecture are miraculously united, in even the smallest details.

Left: Maestro Thierry W. Despont.
Right: The outdoor room adjoining the living area, which can be closed off with a large wooden shutter door.

Above: The front of the Bahamas house designed by Thierry Despont. It is a generously proportioned holiday retreat with the living areas on the left and the passageway to the bedrooms on the right. The hand-blown glass spears were made by Robert DuGrenier Associates Inc., Vermont.

Below: The bedroom section of the house at daybreak; tucked away in a dune among lush vegetation and palm trees. In the background, the majestic ocean. Right: the house at nightfall, giving a good impression of the two separate sections: left, the living spaces and right, the bedroom part.

Next pages:

The living room in Despont style with a spacious passageway leading to the equally spacious terraces. The interior was designed with attetion to every last detail. The kitchen, with a rectangular table, is to the left of the living area.

The plane takes off from Fort Lauderdale in an easterly direction. It flies quite low over a totally fascinating scene in every imaginable shade of blue and turquoise, a picture that seems to have been captured beneath a gigantic glass dome. Occasionally a boat's white wake interrupts the hallucination with reality.

This is the area of the ocean where the islands of the Bahamas are situated—a group of 700 islands and 2,000 cays or keys, of which only around 40 are inhabited. Hardly surprising, therefore, that the sandy beaches and clear waters hold a magical appeal for vacationers. In 1973 the islands gained independence from Great Britain and since then have been a member of the British Commonwealth.

On one of the islands, Thierry W. Despont was commissioned to build a holiday residence that proves to merge extraordinarily well into the landscape of sand dunes, palm trees, and indigenous vegetation. The house actually comprises of two volumes beneath pitched roofs connected by a passageway. It is a symphony of wood and stone, which is demonstrated from the front door on.

"I see myself as a dreamer of houses. I want to make beautiful houses and interiors, but certainly no fancy statements," according to Despont—architect, interior designer and artist—who confirms that adage time and again in his projects in the United States and countries much farther afield.

The Bahamas house nestles in the dunes leading to startlingly white beaches. It is not large, certainly not by Despont standards, but beautifully proportioned. In fact, the rooms are spacious, partly thanks to the lofty ceilings and floor-to-ceiling windows. The interior is a composition of timeless luxury and comfort, in a deliberate mixture of furniture he designed himself plus local accessories. The rooms flow together logically: from the entrance with garden room and living room/kitchen, through a corridor to the wing with the master bedroom and children's rooms. The appointments and color palette can to some extent be accounted for by his "French-ness"—both timeless and titillating, unexpected and responsive to the genius loci. He trained as an architect in his home country, but his move to the United States provided him with the scope to push the confines of his profession to include interior design, landscaping, plus the design of furniture, light fittings and other interior accessories. Nowadays he

Above: The house created on the Bahamas by Thierry Despont is a celebration of tastefully designed details: the terrace, master bedroom, children 's room, dining area in the kitchen, and the outdoor areas.

Right: The living room seen at sunset—right, the kitchen-dining area, and, in the background, the passage to the main entrance and the outdoor area.

has a hard time defining where architecture ends and interior design begins, since the two are inseparable for him. His work revolves around light, volumes, and colors—areas in which he achieves the height of perfection.

In 2008, to mark his 60th birthday, he published a 600-page book filled with his works, varying from private residences to interiors of art galleries, the building of an entire synagogue in the heart of Manhattan, as well as renovations of famous hotels like the Peninsula and the Crillon in Paris and 45 Park Lane (Dorchester) in London. One of his first commissions after he arrived, almost penniless, in New York in 1980 was a curious one: the restoration, in conjunction with another architect, of one of the New World's most evocative icons: the

Previous pages:
The entrance to the house is an early indication of the spacious-ness to be expected inside, something for which Thierry Despont is world famous. All the details have been thought out carefully and together form a logical whole: from the large pivoting front door and solid wooden up-and-over door accessing the exterior space, to the color of the Pyrolave lava stone wall of the pantry. That room contains an OTD custom teak dining table and chairs by VCA. The hanging lamp is by Jeff Taylor for Tama Gallery, NY, and the antique hardwood console is from VCA, MA. The ceiling fan is by Boffi. Lamps and console came from Ms. Mae's, Bahamas, and the lampshades are from Broome Lampshade, NY. The pivoting shutter frame and mechanism is by Jamestown Bronze Works, NY.

These pages:
The house at nightfall with the exterior space (left), and beside that the living and kitchen areas, and the volume contain-ing the bedrooms (right).
Next page:
Part of the master bathroom. The glass objects are by Angel des Montagnes, France, and the handmade satin nickel vanity mirror and sconces by Metalurges, MA. The hanging lamp is by Lisa Kim for Tama Gallery, NY.

Statue of Liberty. The statue, which was originally intended to stand at the entrance to the Suez Canal, but was not finished in time, had been installed in New York in 1886, and was in urgent need of restoration. The 46-meter high statue, weighing 225 tons, was presented by France to the United States to commemorate the centennial of the signing of the Declaration of Independence. It was designed by the French sculptor, Frédéric Bartholdi and is entirely clad in copper plate on a supporting frame designed by Gustave Eiffel. The crown has seven spikes or rays which symbolize the seven continents and seven seas. The 47-metre tall pedestal was made from Euville limestone after a design by the American sculptor, Richard Morris Hunt.

Despont: "It was a fascinating project because no-one knew in advance how to tackle it. Perhaps my French origins were what qualified me for the job." At all events, he made a success of it and thus acquired the credentials that led to his break-through and so made his dreams come true. "I wanted to design houses, and America seemed the place to do it. Here they still build real houses. You have a sense of free-dom here; you can implement ideas and do what you like. People here aren't afraid to make mistakes. It's a bit like 17th-century France. Then, they were discovering and building new things, and they also made mistakes in architecture—but they learnt from their mistakes and didn't let it stop them."

He commented on his profession: "The nice thing about architecture is that you never stop learning. I know what I want to build and, with the benefit of experience, it becomes easier to create attractive things. It's important for me to have a client who knows what he wants. It's very satisfying to work with people like Bill Gates or Calvin Klein: the more forceful the client, the better I can work.

There's never been a 'great' house without a 'great' principal—a strong patron. When someone like that has faith in you as an architect or designer, you can achieve splendid things. There is an interaction, in which the one stimulates the other. Yes, I find it fascinating to create homes for very different characters. It generates diversity, attuned to the client's personality."

This is a diversity that is not subject to trends, but is imbued with enduring, intrinsic beauty. That qualifi-cation certainly applies to the Bahamas island house, the proportions of which are in perfect harmony with its natural surroundings. They bear witness to Thierry Despont's respect for the human scale—Despont, an artist who is able to create beauty out of nothing.

Left: Decorative details, including Bubinga wood table from Les Migrateurs, NY, wooden trumpet vases from Crate and Barrel Home, and a hand-carved tulip poplar bowl from Tama Gallery, NY.

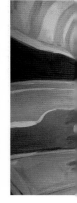

Above: The master bedroom overlooking the large terrace with the ocean beyond. The coral lamps were purchased at a Sotheby's auction. The perforated metal lamp dates from c. 1940 and came from Johnson & Hicks, NY. The shade was made by Broome Lampshade, NY. The sea grass rug is from AM Collections, NY. The OTD custom teak bed frame was supplied by VCA, MA.

Below: Details from the master bedroom. The master bedroom with a glass sculpture by Robert DuGrenier, NY, and the striking partition—designed by Thierry Despont—between bed and boudoir. The Step Tansu cabinet is from Jacques Carcanagues Gallery, NY. The large murals are by Mark Beard, NY. Also, a detail of the solid wooden shutter doors, custom made for the house by Michael Reilly Design, NY, and Byrne Millwork, DE.

The living room at nightfall with a Butterfly chair
from Melet Mercantile, NY, Alvar Aalto dining chairs
from Sotheby's auction house, a teak console table
from Adrianna Shamaris, NY, and an Edward Wormley
party server cart from Wyeth, NY.
The custom finish is by VCA, MA. Tama Gallery, NY, supplied the oxblood lamps, and the antique Indian wa-
terwheel is from Jacques Caranagues Gallery, NY.

RIJKSMUSEUM AMSTERDAM

The Rijksmuseum in Amsterdam and the most

famous museum in the Netherlands reopened after

an all-encompassing restoration and

reorganization which lasted a long ten years.

The metamorphosis of the historic building and

the rearrangement of the world reknown works of art

and the best of Dutch heritage can, without reservation,

be termed spectacular.

It is a shrine of the arts which,

considering the jubilant reviews, is clearly one

of the most beautiful in the world.

Left: In the gallery of honor the decorations on the arches and ceilings have been restored to their former glory. *The Night Watch* can be seen at the head of the gallery of honor. On the left a painting by Jan Asselijn, *The Threatened Swan*, dating from 1650.
The painting was the first acquisition for the Nationale Kunstgalerij (National Art Gallery), the predecessor of the Rijksmuseum. It was purchased for a hundred guilders in 1800.

Above: The painting representing the civic guard known as *De Magere Compagnie* (the Meagre Company) by Frans Hals and Pieter Codde. Height 209 cm.

Below: The new atrium designed by the Spanish architects Ortiz and Cruz is the museum's central entrance hall. Right page, bottom left: Looking through theatrium with, left, the Laocoön sculpture group which once adorned the gardens of the late-18th century Pavilion Welgelegen in Haarlem.

The Rijksmuseum collection comprises over a million items, including pieces stored in the catacombs and other museum storage facilities. Literally everything has been relocated. Only one artwork has returned to the place in the museum envisaged by the architect Pierre Cuypers in 1885: at the head of the gallery of honor. Here hangs Rembrandt's most famous—and largest—masterpiece: the *Night Watch*. The ultimate pièce de résistance and the pinnacle of the gallery of honor, where, in open side-galleries, works by Johannes Vermeer, Frans Hals, Rembrandt, Jan Steen, Willem Claesz Heda, Ruisdael, and other Golden Age celebrities occupy prominent places.

In the past all the museum's interior walls had been painted white. They are now a shade of grey and that, combined with subtle LED lighting, presents the works of art to full advantage. This color scheme, in five shades of grey, has been applied in all the galleries and proves to harmonize remarkably well with all the objects on display.

The Spanish architects Antonio Ortiz and Antonio Cruz designed the new entrance hall with the central atrium, the glass roofing which permits natural light to enter. In the atrium, the chandelier structures are a useful source of light. They also break up the height and muffle noise, which benefits the acoustics in the vast space.

The two architects in close collaboration with the Dutch restoration architect, Gijsbert van Hoogevest, returned the museum to its original relative proportions. Since it was opened 1885, parts of the building had gradually been

Top left: One of the favorites among the museum's visitors: Johannes Vermeer's *View of houses in Delft*, also known as *The Little Street*, painted around 1658. The painting was acquired in 1921 by Sir Henry Deterding (director of Shell) for 625,000 guilders and donated to the Rijksmusem.
Top right: The self-portrait of Vincent van Gogh painted in 1887 is the only Van Gogh owned by the museum. It has been framed in appropriate style by the Haarlem-based Ateliers de Roo.
Below right: Johannes Vermeer's *Milkmaid* (1660)—another favourite with the public—hangs in the Rijkmuseum's gallery of honour.

Bottom left: An unusual painter's box from the 17th century, contains pigments, paint mixing tray, and other attributes.

Bottom right: Looking through the William & Mary gallery where early 18th-century Delft pottery and furniture with inlaid intarsia are on display. Far left: An imposing Delft flower pyramid or tulip vase one-and-a-half meters in height, ca. 1700.

In the foreground, two Delft jugs and a Delft pottery birdcage.

Right page, bottom: A selection of early Delft blue, including two vases with chinoiserie décor, ca. 1700.

Far left: A two-door, intarsia cabinet (ca. 1695-1710) inlaid with a veneer of fine woods by Jan van Mekeren; the doors are decorated with flowers in a vase pattern.

Right: The fighter plane, the FK 23 Bantam biplane, dating from 1917 and designed by Frits Koolhoven. It was acquired in 2011 and is the oldest preserved Dutch plane.

boarded up and the museum had become a dark, gloomy labyrinth. In the course of the last century, in what had originally been open spaces, numerous new rooms and side-galleries had been created to accommodate the steadily expanding art collection. As a result, authentic frescoes, decorations, and stained glass windows were hidden behind double walls.

The radical restoration—costing in the end 375 million euros—has revealed more about the building itself, the partial Gothic revival and Renaissance style of architecture and the concomitant decorations. It was even possible to reconstruct the mosaic-terrazzo floors using the original design drawings.

The French architect Jean-Michel Wilmotte was responsible for redesigning the interiors of the exhibition galleries and creating the non-reflective glass display cabinets. Now the building's 19th-century grandeur combines subtly with modern design. However, the protagonist will always be the world-renowned art collection housed in the museum.

The Rijksmuseum has not only had a cosmetic facelift, it has undergone a complete thematic metamorphosis. In regular museums you are confronted, gallery after gallery, with paintings, religious sculptures, collections of porcelain or silver, and other items that are arranged according to theme or class. A surfeit—too much—the same. In the new Rijksmuseum a different formula has been chosen. Everything is presented chronologically, starting in the early Middle Ages. History and art are combined in lively fashion. Today paintings are hung close to the actual objects they depict, making the overall presentation and disposition far more animated and creating interaction between fine and decorative art. Famous Dutch still-lifes from the 17th century hang beside the characteristic greenish roemer glasses and blue-and-white Chinese porcelain portrayed in the paintings; costly furniture, glass- and silverware illustrate the prosperity that prevailed during the Dutch Golden Age.

In addition, the seafaring nation of the Netherlands is visualized by way of maritime paintings, arms, ship models, other models, and objects from the former colonies. Costumes, portraits, and jewellery reflect the changing view on lifestyle and fashion through the centuries. Accordingly, Dutch history and culture in their numerous facets are illustrated in unexpected ways.

The permanent museum display extends through eighty galleries and four floors where some 8,000 artworks and objects have found a place. The top floor houses modern and contemporary art, photography, posters, furniture designs by the Dutch architect Gerrit Rietveld, and a fighter plane from 1917, the largest item in the museum collection.

Above: The original mosaic and terrazzo floors in the forehall and upstairs hallway have been meticulously reconstructed in accordance with architect Pierre Cuypers's design drawings from 1885.
Right: The monumental library, designed in 1885 by Pierre Cuypers, is now open to the public for the first time. The library also has a reading room where, on request, visitors can look at, and study prints, drawings, and old editions.

Below: A partially painted and gilded Guanyin figure, over one meter in height; Shanxi, China, 12th century. For centuries the statue stood in a Buddhist temple.

Below left: Partially polychrome wooden statue from the 16th century of a 2-year-old Japanese statesman. He is depicted at prayer to indicate that even at that tender age he had religious awareness and worshipped Buddha.

Beside that: Exterior of the new Asian Pavilion designed by the Spanish architects, Cruz and Ortiz, seen from the garden side.

Below right: A bronze Shiva Nataraja depicted as the king of dance, India, 12th century.
Height: 153 cm.

Right page: A series of five portraits (almost 2 meters in height) of Javanese court officials in garments with batik motifs. They were painted by an anonymous, non-Western artist in the first half of the 19th century. In the foreground, a diorama of a village scene in the former Dutch East Indies.

Although the protracted work on the 19th-century national monument related primarily to renovation and restoration, a new segment was also added to the museum. On the south side of the original museum building, the two-storey Asian Pavilion, part of which is underground, has been created. It is built in Portuguese sandstone and glass, and is surrounded by water.

The many oblique surfaces and unusual sight-lines characterize this new accommodation for the important collection of Asian art originating in particular from China, Vietnam, and Thailand, Japan, Indonesia, and India. The exhibits date from 2000 BC to the present day. Inside, one of the eye-catchers is a 300-kilo bronze sculpture of the dancing Hindu god, Shiva Nataraja, dating from the 12th century. It was once carried in processions and symbolized both creation and destruction. This version portrays Shiva as the king of dance. The gallery, with its serene atmosphere, also contains a selection of Indian and Indonesian statues.

One floor below is the collection of (art) objects from China, Japan, and Korea. Here you are confronted by two, somewhat terrifying wooden Japanese temple guardians, some 2.5 meters in height. The two "heavenly guardians," Ungyo and Agyo, are recent acquisitions. Only a few pieces from the splendid Asian porcelain collection are on show. When asked, the curator was to explained that the display will be changed at frequent intervals.

The entrance to the impressive library is situated near the Asian Pavilion. It is open to the public for the first time in its history. Here, on request, you can consult antiquarian books, examine portfolios of drawings and prints from the museum collection, or leaf through museum catalogues. The library is part of the Print Room which manages by far the most items of the museum collection: some 700,000 works on paper.

Huigen Leeflang, curator of the Print Room, explained that the current museum policy makes it possible for several small presentations of their collection of drawings and prints to be held simultaneously at different locations in the museum. It is possible not only to enjoy 16th-century paintings, but also drawings and prints from the same period.

It is evident that the recently reopened Rijksmuseum is a mega-crowd puller, both of international and Dutch visitors. The museum expects around two million visitors each year.
It also sets great store by interesting young people in art and culture. The museum is open to the public 365 days a year and has free admission for everyone under the age of 18. At the opening, the director of the Rijksmuseum, Wim Pijbes, vividly expressed the intention of the institute (which the Rijksmuseum is, after all).
"A museum should tell stories and be an adventure." Every visitor will agree, they have certainly succeeded.

Right: *The Night Watch*, Rembrandt's master-piece dating from 1642, hangs again in its original spot—the only work in the museum to be returned to its old place.
Night Watch depicts the officers and other civic guardsmen of district II, under the command of Captain Frans Banninck Cocq and Lieutenant Willem van Ruytenburgh. The painting measures 363 by 437 cm.
Originally it was bigger, but at the start of the 18th century, it was cut down on the left and right sides to fit at a specific location in what was then the Town Hall on Dam Square.

ART BESIDE AN
AMSTERDAM CANAL

It's a typical Amsterdam canal house, with large,

high windows on the lower floors and sturdy

wooden beams.

This is home to Arty Grimm and Miguel Ybáñez

and they have given it a thorough makeover,

transforming it into an "art house."

It takes stamina to restore and remodel a canal house in the historic heart of the Dutch city of Amsterdam—as well as a good helping of ideological enthusiasm. The countless rules and regulations that are in force, even regarding the specific color of the front door, can make tremendous demands on the owner's nerves. Various committees and government agencies watch with eagle eyes to ensure the renovations are not too enthusiastic. The artists Arty Grimm and Miguel Ybáñez steered a course around the regulations and succeeded in fulfilling their personal interpretation of the terms "interior renovation" and "decoration".

The premises, bought in 2008, are at the Keizersgracht. The artists found two identical buildings along the canal that were built around 1700 and in recent decades were home to two ladies. When they purchased one of the two houses, the interior comprised a maze of small rooms divided over six storeys. Nowhere were doors higher than 1.80 meters and the steep staircases would have challenged even a skillfull mountaineer.

A special feature of the existing premises was the deep garden at the back, including a garden house. There are many such hidden garden treasures in Amsterdam where rural peace and quiet prevail and towering trees provide shade. The existing garden house was to be their home during the building operations. More windows—sourced from a greenhouse north of the Netherlands—were added for additional comfort. Their friend, the designer Arno Twigt, got a blacksmith to make additional panelling.

The first obstacle in the renovation was the basement. As soon as water had been pumped out, it gushed back beneath the vaults. That suggested a connecting river must once have flowed here between Keizersgracht and Herengracht canals. Whole batches of cement were poured on the newly pile-supported underlying structure to keep the tsunami from flooding in. That serious intervention created a solid foundation for the implementation of the renovation plans. Today, you enter through this basement which, at the rear, leads via a small studio right through to the garden.

Left: The garden house. It served as the family home while the canal house was being transformed for them.
Above: The stairs that connects the lower floors. Arty and Miguel managed to create an open staircase in the middle of the house, without compromising the old structure.

Overleaf:
The sitting in the kitchen overlooking the garden.

 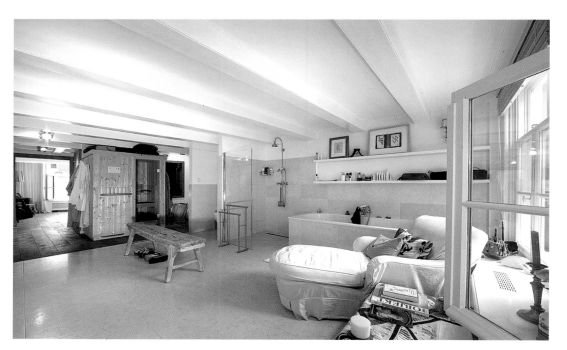

Above: The master bedroom at the front and the bathroom at the back on the third floor of the house.

Right: Like many of the Amsterdam canal houses, the one belonging to Miguel and Arty has a very deep back garden. Here, the sounds of the city are muffled and tall trees provide shade in the summer.

Overleaf:

The kitchen-living room at the back of the house. The long L-shaped unit along the wall is one of the few items that stays in place: the rest of the furniture is regularly shifted around.

All the walls and beams on the floors above were scraped bare and from that *tabula rasa* Arty and Miguel developed their plans, within the framework of the statutory regulations. They managed to create an open staircase in the middle of the house without compromising the old structure. So it was possible to get rid of the original narrow, steep stairs. Starting from that central newel, each storey could be tackled in turn.

One prerequisite was to create sufficient rooms and transitional spaces to house the large artworks in fitting fashion. The floor above the basement is now a large living room with, at the canal side, a reading table surrounded by upright and arm chairs. At the back there is a kitchen-living space with a huge L-shaped worktop and, on the other side, a large round table with cheerful benches and industrial chairs. Miguel created a "heavenly" painting on the ceiling and the walls are decorated with a variety of packaging proofs and graphic paintings by the two artists themselves.

The disposition of the furniture is highly flexible: Arty likes constant change, as well as being an almost compulsive collector of things that are also always being moved around. "The whole house keeps getting clogged up. I have a weakness for 'stuff' and love to collect things," Arty explained. On the first floor at the canal side, a library-cum-video room has been made, and at the back there is a bedroom for guests. Above that is the master bedroom at the front of the house. A generous bathroom is located at the back. There is evidence of Arty's passion for collecting throughout. It actually goes amazingly well with the interior style: luxuriously nonchalant and, above all, comfortable.

Wherever you look there is art, mostly by Arty and Miguel themselves. Art is their livelihood. They have a big studio at walking distance from their home, in a street between the canals. "Miguel is totally absorbed in his art. I wouldn't want to do without my work either, but I still have time for other things I enjoy. Travel, my grandchildren, reading, my friends: I devote half my time to them. I pick up the phone and organize things," energetic Arty Grimm told us. She has a strong preference for the city life, whereas Miguel works alone for long periods in the seclusion of their farm in the north of Spain. Arty's work is mainly painting, while much of Miguel's ranges over the art kaleidoscope: from paintings to sculpture and from bronzes to ceramics.

FORM FOLLOWS WIND

It's the biggest balloon festival in the world—the Balloon Fiesta of Albuquerque, New Mexico. The plethora of flying objects besieging the skies flouts all the principles of aviation. No sophisticated aerodynamics and streamlined designs here, but the most amazing shapes navigating the remarkable Albuquerque Box. OBJEKT©International scrambled into the basket beneath Ham-Let the Flying Pig and sailed over the Rio Grande, to end up bumping down into a residential area.

These pages: The Balloon Fiesta of Albuquerque in the United States. Here, the "Special Shapes" take to the air during the 2007 event. This is part of a gigantic show involving 750 hot-air balloons, plus balloonists and chase teams.
Top left: Three Brazilian balloons: Jairo Fogaca's pink Mr. Puwp, Eduardo de Mello's yellow Mr. Scarecrow, and the Haunted House belonging to Antonio Marques. Below that: the Purple People Eater piloted by John Cavin from the United States and Ham-Let, the world's biggest flying pig, at sunset.
Top right: Brazilian Mauro Chemin's Airplane Happy with, behind it, Farmer Pig operated by Luiz Paulo Assis, also from Brazil.
Bottom right: Darth Vader by Jean-Michel and Benoit Lambert of Belgium, and Dale Ritchie's enormous flying cow, Airabelle.

Top left: The end of the Special Shapes flight early in the morning in an Albuquerque residential district.
Top right: The Balloon Glow, a spectacular daily event that takes place at sunset.
When officials send a signal, pilots of the Albuquerque Balloon Fiesta's Special Shape balloons simultaneously light the burners, thus illuminating their balloons. This photo features several balloons, including the Warsteiner Orient Express and the Brandenburg Gate from Germany, flanked by Hazelnut and Sunny Boy from the United States and the Possman Bembel from Germany.
Far right: An entire tree trunk complete with birds—Gary Moore's Woodrow C. Greenleaf—flying alongside the world's biggest flying pig Ham-Let.
Ham-Let owned by Douglas Gantt, hosted the OBJEKT©International team and gave them a ride during this event.
The river below is the famous Rio Grande.

Every October the elite of the ballooning world descends on a field just outside the American town of Albuquerque, New Mexico. There, in the shadow of the Anderson-Abruzzo International Balloon Museum, the ballooning jet set navigate, with their hot-air balloons, the wind patterns of the famous Albuquerque Box that prevail on October mornings.

It is a unique meteorological situation, in which stable, opposing wind flows occur at varying heights. It enables pilots to alter altitude, leaving the balloon park in one direction and pursuing the box shape to return at a higher altitude.
The "box" phenomenon was the original reason for the world's biggest ballooning festival, the Balloon Fiesta, in which some 750 teams take part. The Special Shapes category is a unique attraction. These hot-air balloons are made in the most fantastic shapes that have little, if anything, to do with aerodynamics. The design concept is based purely on the fun factor. Functionality does not come into it; all that matters is the shape. In design circles the products would be sneered at, but for this special occasion the effect is stunning.
OBJEKT©International clocked in bright and early. The balloon grounds were still shrouded in darkness and it was cold.

Once the first balloonists arrived on the field with their materials and auxiliary forces, everything proceeded quickly. Huge expanses of fabric were unrolled, ventilators and propellers started up and the first tentative shapes began to lift off the ground. A whole succession of designs were taking shape. Gondolas with gas burners were attached and soon, at a sign from the "zebras" the launch officials first balloons took to the skies.

The OBJEKT team climbed into a kind of mulberry laundry basket suspended beneath Ham-Let, the world's biggest Flying Pig.
It is imperative to wear protective headgear, to prevent the heat from the huge burners singeing your hair.
Pilot Douglas Gantt explained how his pig originated, quoting the answer his father would give him when, as a child, he asked for something special. Father would write him off with, "When pigs fly." It led Douglas to construct the enormous flying pig, in which the Ham-Let team today travels from one event to another.
OBJEKT's flight passed over the Rio Grande, accompanied left and right, above and below, by the most outlandish shapes. Eventually it landed in a residential development where the chase teams were waiting to roll up the vast lengths of material and return to base.

VIEW OF A CALIFORNIAN SURFERS' PARADISE

The house is situated high in a hillside of the town of Ventura, just

north of Los Angeles along the Pacific Ocean.

This has long been a paradise for surfers and artists.

Designer Philip Nimmo has conjured up a highly distinctive

vision of the modern living theme here.

He designed an open-plan house with large expanses of glass,

terraces at the front and rear and even on the roof

of the master bedroom.

His creation draws upon outdoor living, with

the ever-changing light as the dynamic catalyst.

Above: Designer Philip Nimmo from Los Angeles.
Right: The floating staircase accesses the roomy roof terrace. The master bedroom is seen here at a somewhat lower level.

Overleaf
The terrace at the front of the house overlooking the Pacific Ocean. The loungers are by Summit. All outdoor fabrics are by Perennials.

Above: The kitchen serves as a passage to the outdoor terrace where there is a dining bar and outdoor kitchen. An almost invisible wall separates interior and exterior. The chairs are by Sutherland and the large Nigel Dragon chandelier is from Hudson Furniture. Right: The roof terrace on top of the master bedroom. The furniture are by Sutherland.

The house sits like a white pearl against a hillside near the town of Ventura on the Pacific Coast north of Los Angeles. Here Philip Nimmo has created a modern house inspired by the architecture of the mid-20th century. His design is based on a seamless transition from interior to exterior. He has achieved that with large expanses of glass on almost all sides. The house is built on a projecting site, so the architect made appropriate provisions for protection from the wind. Despite local building regulations for this spot, he succeeded in subtly stretching them to the limit in order to meet all the owners' requirements. Much of the existing structure was replaced with new-build, though a detached element was retained—it houses the entertainment room and garage.

In the tautly designed new-build, Philip has placed the large living-cum-dining space in an efficient manner. It flows into the kitchen with a connecting space to the outdoor kitchen and dining table at the back of the house.

At the front he designed the living room to abut a terrace, which has a small pool and waterfall. The large glass wall can be opened electronically to create a spacious indoor/outdoor area. From the outdoor terrace a floating staircase leads to a large open-air terrace on top of the master bedroom. That bedroom with roomy en suite bathroom, is sunken behind the living area. The house contains two bedrooms and bathrooms, as well as a multipurpose study. A major item in the brief was for sufficient wall space to accommodate

Next pages:

The living room with the integrated dining room in the background and the kitchen beyond that. The kitchen continues into an outdoor kitchen and alfresco dining area. Thanks to the many expanses of glass, daylight can enter freely into the interior and, during daytime, forms an ever-changing pattern of shadows. The tree sculpture is by Holly Hunt and the sofa by Philip Nimmo. Above the dining table (which has chairs by Philip Nimmo), is a lighting fixture by Fuse Lighting. The painting behind the dining table is by Jennifer Wolf.

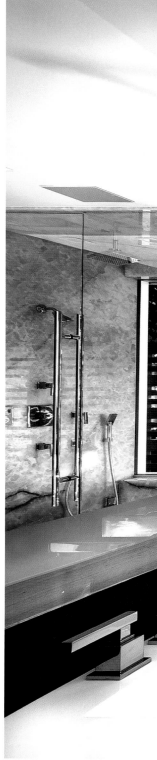

Above: The guest bathroom as a symphony of clear-cut lines, prominently veined red marble sinks, with an extra red accent provided by the artwork by Remy Wong.
Right: The bathroom for the master bedroom with a view through to the garden. Taps by Newport Brass, Amsterdam chairs by James Magni, and Swarovski table by Gary Hutton.

the owners' art. Ramsey Construction played a key role in realizing the designer's highly subtle plans. They were responsible for the meticulous degree of finish and chose a sophisticated lighting plan for the house.

"I tried to design a maximum of wall space for the works by young artists from California from the owners' collection. To avoid upsetting the spatial effect, we kept the ceilings as high as possible. Within that context, we opted for furniture with both architectural and sculptural properties. The color palette for the furniture was mainly neutral with the occasional accent color for cushions and accessories", Philip Nimmo explained.

Although the house is not particularly large by American standards, the great transparency Nimmo has created makes it appear far more spacious. That is reinforced by the emphasis on outdoor living. The climate permits the pleasant alfresco life for much of the year, and when all the picture windows are open, there is a feeling of infinity.

And with the natural light creating a dynamic exchange between light and shade during the day, the effect is further enhanced. The panoramic view of the ocean heightens even more the sense of unlimited space.

Next pages:
The somewhat sunken bedroom is located at a corner of the house and also has picture windows, meaning that there is a good view of the ocean from the bed. Side tables are by Philip Nimmo Ironworks, the bed itself was designed by Philip Nimmo, the bedside lamps are by Blackman Cruz, the chair in the background is by Moura Starr, and the rug is from Mansour.

THE ULTIMATE CONSEQUENCE OF VISUAL SYMMETRY

The house stands like a large white beacon on top of a cliff at

Coral Estate, a high end development project on the southwest

coast of the Caribbean island of Curaçao.

It is an ode to symmetry: classical architecture with a modern

thrust. It was designed by the man who has put Dutch interior

design on the map and has won international acclaim

as a furniture designer: Jan des Bouvrie.

This page: The house built by Dutch designer Jan des Bouvrie on the Caribbean island of Curaçao. It has been created as a veritable source of indoor-outdoor delight with a pool as an extension of the living areas.

Jan des Bouvrie is a phenomenon in the Netherlands, and far beyond. He started out in the 1960s as a furniture designer and has done much to boost interior design—something he continues to do today.

He made his breakthrough with the Cube sofa for furniture manufacturers Gelderland, a design which still has contemporary appeal and celebrated its 40th anniversary in 2009 in lavish style.

At Het Arsenaal, an old munitions depot in Naarden (one of the best preserved fortified towns in Europe and famous for its unique star shape), Jan des Bouvrie and his wife Monique present their approach to the interior.

Het Arsenaal is neither a home furnishing store nor a furniture showroom, but rather an ongoing, changing exhibition featuring furniture and art as a source of inspiration in the interior.

Above: Tranparency is king: the interior follows a completely symmetrical pattern, starting from the kitchen in the foreground which forms the hub of the house, occupying the entire width of the living area.
Right: Monique and Jan des Bouvrie.

This image gives a good impression of the open character of the des Bouvrie house in Curaçao. By opening the glass doors completely, a flowing totality is created of terraces, living area, kitchen, and patio beyond. All the furniture and further accessories were designed by Jan des Bouvrie. Beneath the bar, LEDs make for changing colors.

But today Jan des Bouvrie also specializes increasingly in architecture, starting from the interior. He describes it as, "Designing the house starting with the chair, as opposed to starting with the outside."

The Caribbean island of Curaçao has provided him with the opportunity to do just that. "Curaçao is an island you either like or dislike. I like it. It's relatively easy to build something attractive. The Dutch architect Gerrit Rietveld executed several fine buildings there. I often used to sit in the morning, drawing, and ideas on verandas and on the flow of interior to exterior would just come to me. And that combined with my assumption that the kitchen is the heart of every house. On Curaçao I had the opportunity to realize those designs, and I've been developing the ideas further in Holland and abroad."

On Curaçao, des Bouvrie encountered the architecture of the imposing mansions in Scharlooweg, once one of the finest architectural statements of the entire Caribbean. Most of the majestic houses were built at the end of the 19th century, and many have been restored to their former glory. He was inspired by the compositions of steps, galleries, and patios and their alignment with respect to the trade winds. They were to form the basis for his drawings and floor plans of projects, which were built on the island under his orchestration.
The designer: "To me, Cuaraçao will always be the island where I learned to build, where I discovered the real purpose of a veranda. It not only provides protection against the sun, but also against wind and rain."

These pages: Two of the bedrooms with en suite bathroom. Here again, the color white predominates—an important constant in Jan des Bouvrie's work. In his designs all the bedrooms have their own bathrooms.
The large outdoor terrace merges seamlessly into the all white interior.

Left: A part of the living room with outside view to both sides of the house.
Below: Bird's eye view of the ultimate consequence of visual symmetry

Next pages:
The long swimming pool at dusk. This gives a clear picture of the way the various rooms interrelate and how indoors and outdoors merge together effortlessly.

Jan des Bouvrie: "At Coral Estate I got the chance to realize an overall concept in which I designed everything from the architecture down to the smallest details. In fact, that's what all the grand masters did in the past: My ultimate dream is to realize that idea about the overall architecture and interior design in St. Tropez on the French Mediterranean coast. That's where Monique and I feel most at home."

He continues: "I've always been good at making floor plans that tally. And that applies in this house. It's pleasant to walk through, you don't have any feeling of irritation. It's like walking round a Porsche: everything in the design tallies. I chose a mode of construction that enabled me to express the pure form, as I once did with my Cube sofa. The outdoor terrace merges seamlessly into the interior. The positioning of the bedrooms that are set symmetrically has created a patio at the back, which is also a logical part of the whole," the designer explained, adding: "For me, a house must always have a soul. You have to live there together, but everyone must have their own place. For instance, I always create personal spaces where you can be yourself in peace. Also, in my designs all the bedrooms have their own bathrooms. These are all elements that add up to a 'fresh' house, like this one and all my other residential projects."

Above: The spacious sitting area looking through to the dining area and kitchen beyond. The travertine floors, which run throughout the space, serve as a connecting element. Large windows overlook the garden with swimming pool, and the adjacent woods. Some of the outdoor furniture was still stored away when this photo was taken at the end of winter. The indoor sofas are by Roche Bobois. Right: the back of the house plus swimming pool on a summer's day.

THE LOOK-THROUGH BOX
OF MONTREAL

The house is tucked away among the trees on the

edge of Lorraine Wood just outside the Canadian

city of Montreal.

It was designed by Renée Daoust of Daoust Lestage

who built it for friends (the founders of the Shan

fashion brand).

It is a modern, open house, in which almost all the

rooms downstairs and on the first floor are open-plan;

a striking, taut presence in a residential suburb,

where the architectural style

is both indescribable and inconsistent.

The tautly designed, L-shaped house is on the very edge of Lorraine Wood, a half-hour's drive from Montreal. It is a suburban setting, bathed in the greenery of the trees. Most houses in the neighborhood were built along traditional—somewhat uninspiring—lines, making Renée Daoust's creation stand out all the more. It is a house of intelligent and sober design, the prerequisite being transparency. Large glass window walls run from floor to roof encased in walls of grey stone.

At the front and at the short side of the L-shape, the architect has placed the garage and entrance hall, followed by the toilet and washrooms. In the hall, large mirrors reflect views of the garden planted with a row of trees. The hall leads straight into the spacious living area, which contains almost all the living functions. On one side, the kitchen (designed by

Renée Daoust and Chantal Levesque and based on Poliform elements) takes up practically the entire width of the volume. A wide kitchen island serves as a bar and breakfast table. The height at the centre of the space soaring roof-wards, creates an atrium with the master bedroom on one side and the study on the other.

At ground level there is a formal dining room, which in turn adjoins the roomy sitting area. At the street side of this space there are elegant staircases leading to the floors above and below. On the woodland side, high glass window walls allow the interior to engage with the imposing natural surroundings and the swimming pool area. There is a profusion of daylight flooding in on either side and it is cast back by the pale travertine floor, thus cutting the need for artificial light to a minimum.

Above: The architect Renée Daoust at the front of the house. Landscaping by Stuart Webster Design.
Right: The house seen from the street; it is in a suburb of Lorraine, a small town just outside Montreal.

Right page: the dining area in the middle of the open layout.

The future occupants had an important requirement for Renée Daoust of Daoust Lestage of Montreal: they wanted to create a transparent totality, but still have the feeling of intimacy. A house in which the different spaces would achieve synergy. The various interior and exterior elements were to interact and thus reinforce one another. Renée drew up a plan with variable vertical screens which would provide the right degree of intimacy. The design of the master bedroom is also unusual: it resembles a box floating in the large space. Here again, transparency is the key, from the shower zone which is placed right behind the entrance, to the open sink, with, looking between and beyond the mirrors, a direct view of the bedroom. The large surrounding window walls make a direct interplay with nature.

Above and left: The master bedroom overlooking the woods as well as the lower floor. On the other side of the atrium there is a study. The bathroom is open plan and has a shower at the front and sink behind the bath.
Right page: The master bedroom seen from the bathroom. The many mirrors reflect light into the darkest corners. Cabinetry and other joinery is by Segabo Design and Ébinisterie Aktuel. The doors were made by Menuiserie des Pins and window walls by Techniverre.

The ground floor seen from the kitchen. The section in the
middle reaches up to the roof. From the master bedroom
and the study on the other side there is an unimpeded
view of the entire lower floor.
The lighting systems were designed by Sistemalux. The
staircase leading downstairs accesses the children's rooms.
The staircase itself was made by Atelier Tac and the rail-
ings are from À Tout Fer. Vitreco supplied the glazing.

GRIMANESA AMORÓS'
COLORFUL OMNIVERSEM

She was born at the coast of Peru. She lives and works in the land of

her birth, and in New York.

OBJEKT©International visited her in her penthouse and studio in Tribeca,

where she enthusiastically told about her art projects.

Sculpture, video, lighting and sound are interwoven into a totality in

breathtaking works. The interior of her home reflects, in all its exuberance,

the essence of her home land and of her work.

Left: the Peruvian-born artist, Grimanesa Amorós, on the roof terrace of her apartment in Tribeca, Manhattan.
Right: part of the living room.

Overleaf
The upper floor on the Tribeca apartment of Grimanesa Amorós. All the living functions are concentrated in this space. It is a cheerful combination of antique and modern furniture, colours, and artworks she has made herself.
Behind the swing there is a passageway to the kitchen.
The bedrooms are situated at the mezzanine level. Grimanesa made the art objects hanging and standing in the spacious room.

Above: Grimanesa Amorós' Uros House in the corner building in the heart of Tribeca and part of the panoramic view from her roof terrace.

Below: Large sculptures in Times Square. They were part of the Times Square Alliance's Public Art Program/Armory Show.
The ingenious installation took up the ever-changing light of the over-abundant neon signs.
Adjoining: The sitting area in a child's bedroom beside the large living room.

Overleaf
Left: Part of Grimanesa Amorós' apartment, looking through to the kitchen and the lift to the roof terrace.
The decoration, even on the lift shaft, is clearly inspired by her home land. She actually had it made by artists who also make street art like this in the poor neighbourhoods of Lima.
The glass bridge accesses the master bedroom.

Right: The antique lift which is a veritable objet d'art; it is operated manually and is still fully functional.

Tribeca, a neighborhood in Lower Manhattan, has undergone a true metamorphosis in recent decades. Until the mid-20th century it had been an industrial area, the main buildings being warehouses. They are still there, but since the 1970s when artists started moving in, they have gradually acquired a different use.

Things really took off in more recent years and today the neighborhood, whose name is an acronym based on 'Triangle Below Canal Street', is an oasis of restaurants and spacious apartments. The Tribeca Film Festival, initiated by Robert de Niro, has certainly helped to add the neighborhood to New York's 'must-see' places.

Here, at the corner of Hudson Street, above the Issey Miyake store, is where the Peruvian artist Grimanesa Amorós lives with her family. Her apartment is on the top floor; one floor down, the studio is in full swing.

As soon as you enter the brightly painted hallway decorated with large circular objects on the walls and ceiling, it is obvious that you have come to the right place. A lift, dating from the days that the buildings were used as warehouses, is still operated in the old-fashioned way, by pulling on a steel cable to get it moving and to bring it a halt. The lift opens into a space she has fitted out for her daughter and includes a lounge and a dining area.

Antique Peruvian doors access the apartment itself. It is one large space with windows on two sides. In the old ceiling large rectangular rooflights have been inserted serving only to increase the existing profusion of daylight. In a corner of the apartment there is a good-sized kitchen with big windows. She designed the large glass table and the chairs herself in order to accentuate the feeling of transparency. That corner is also where the lift and the stairs are situated, leading to the rooms above and to the large roof terrace.

A glass bridge crosses over the kitchen and leads to the bedrooms. The shaft of the lift, which was installed at a later date, is covered with works by Lima street artists—works that Grimanesa commissioned specially in her home land. The interior of the lift can be used by guests as a visitors book. At the back of the apartment there is a free-standing volume containing all the functional spaces such as toilets and washing facilities.

The roof terrace is spectacular and is divided over several levels: from the lower, more intimate space to the upper level containing a trampoline, there are 360-degree views over New York.

The apartment's living area is a continuous ensemble of spaces, passing the antique dining table with antique chairs through to the succession of sitting zones. The colors have clearly been inspired by Peru, with a large swing decorated with brightly-coloured Peruvian fabrics as a striking feature. Artworks by Grimanesa stand, hang or lie everywhere.

When OBJEKT©International visited her the first time, she was just finishing off some work for the Venice Art Biennale. It comprises large acrylic spheres of highly refined structures which allude to her childhood at the coast of Peru and the sea-scoured stones on the beach.

Her *Uros Island – Lighting Sculpture Installation* is part of *Future Pass*, a project at the 54th art festival curated by Victoria Lu, Felix Schoeber and Renzo di Renzo. After the Biennale, the exhibition went on tour, and be on show at Rotterdam's Wereldmusuem, the National Taiwan Art Museum in Taichung and the Beijing Art Museum in China.

Grimanesa showed photos of her Uros House project at Times Square, where similar spheres form huge sculptures of polyethylene which are illuminated from the ever-changing light of the over-abundant neon signs.

She is an interdisciplinary artist, an all-rounder who uses varying art-forms – including sculpture, light, video and sound – in her work. Her art reflects her views on personal identity and community. It is socially engaged, but with the humour and lightness of her Peruvian roots.

Above: The staircase to the bedroom section designed for Times Square Alliance's Public Art Program/Armory Show. In the centre, the antique table from Peru and, right, the lift (installed later) to the roof terrace. Guests have written stories and poems on the walls. Here, Izabel Fonk adds her contribution.

Right: Part of her *Uros Island – Lighting Sculpture Installation* which featured in the *Future Pass* project at the 54th International Venice Biennale curated by Victoria Lu, Felix Schoeber and Renzo di Renzo. The exhibition could be seen at Fondazione Claudio Buziol, a non-profit, private institute in Venice. After Venice, the exhibition was shown at Rotterdam's Wereldmusuem, the National Taiwan Art Museum in Taichung and the Beijing Art Museum in China

MERCATO
CENTRALE
DI
FIRENZE

Just a stone's throw from the Duomo, Florence's
famous cathedral, another monument has been
restored to its former splendor: the 140-year old
Mercato Centrale (central market). It has been
transformed into a prime culinary destination.
On the ground floor, a huge variety of fresh products
as found in a traditional market setting is on sale.
On the first floor, a tip-top Italian culinary
paradise has been created.
It was an initiative of Umberto Montano, a
well-known catering entrepreneur.
The redevelopment project was handled by
architecture studio Archea Associati of Florence.

Left: Umberto Montano, the initiator of the Mercato Centrale project in the Italian city of Florence. He set the ball rolling for the transformation of the empty first floor of the domain into a culinary paradise.
Above: The Mercato Centrale that forms the vibrant hub of this part of the old city. The dome of the cathedral can be seen in the background.

The Mercato Centrale in the heart of Florence was built around 1874 after a design by Giuseppe Mengoni, who was also the architect of the Galleria Vittorio Emanuele II in Milan. He derived inspiration for the market in Florence from Les Halles in Paris. For the construction he used materials that were current at that time, including steel, glass, and cast iron. Since the renovation of the first floor, the building's structure is once more evident. Florence's Mercato Centrale embodies a highly contemporary and necessary vision: to re-populate a very important area that is vital to the historic center, with a series of newly-conceived services and gourmet shops, designed to spotlight artisans of taste.

With the restored complex, Florence has a new and truly vast indoor space covering 3,000 m^2 populated by shops of some of the best-known Italian artisans, and much more. Open every day for an experience of taste, and fun, Florence's Mercato Centrale is intended as a spacious venue where authenticity, spontaneity, and tradition will be highlighted. People can come and buy, sample, taste, but also discover, listen, read, tell, and be told: because the Mercato Centrale will be a place of cultural interchange, offering a wealth of special buys, activities, and stimuli.

The objective of the project was to focus on excellent foods and wines, and to disseminate some of the city's cultural heritage. Accordingly, Florence now boasts a newly-devised indoor market with contemporary features integrated in the historic Mercato Centrale. The result is the merging of two identities: the traditional, repre-

sented by the stalls on the ground floor with all the charm that has characterized them for 140 years, and the current identity aimed at offering new inspiration as compared with "normal" grocery shopping.

There is a strong focus on the local region, yet this is not all exclusive. There is still room for all the good things that come from else-where. After all, Florence has always been a center that brings together all the cultures of the world.
The challenge was to make that input topical and recognizable. The main steps had been to reinstate the handmade tradition, the true great asset of Italian cuisine, and return to the shops that enable those master craftsmen of flavors to produce their best.
"In addition, it is their task to elaborate on the various fields in which they star: so a market that will be able to tell its own story", Umberto Montano explains. He is a well-known catering entrepreneur (with restaurants Alle Murate and Caffè Italiano) and Florentine by adoption. He was the driving force behind the market project.

Each craftsman involved has in fact accepted strict rules which, in addition to guaranteeing the excellence of their food products, transparency and traceability requires him and his colleagues to explain and transfer their knowledge to the public. In order to document this delicate step from the very start of Florence's Mercato Centrale, a fully-fledged "Quality Passport" has been initiated which underpins the project.

In addition to the gourmet store, a bar and café area have been designed by merging the Caffé Italiano and Flò concepts. Florence's Piansa coffee shop has created an exclusive coffee blend for the Mercato Centrale. For beer lovers, Florence's Mercato Centrale offers a large tasting space

integrations of shops, deploying lightweight and dismountable structures, designed in such a way as to transform the pre-existing space into a theatre of flavors.

"Based upon the 'food-culture' combination, the first floor architecture was triggered by a creative principle: to redevelop one of Italy's most beautiful historic markets by introducing a contemporary use system aimed at meeting the requirements of an increasingly diverse and cultured public. It was not, however, a project that could be confined to the area of interior design but rather a protected architecture designed on a urban scale where the lightness and brightness of the wonderful iron and cast iron framework of the nineteenth-century structure was

for Birra Moretti, an historic brand founded in Udine by Luigi Moretti in 1859. Eataly is also taking part in the project.

Florence's Mercato Centrale will boast an Arclinea Design cooking school, run by the Lorenzo de' Medici Institute of Fabrizio and Carla Guarducci, and a wine-tasting area with wine school entrusted to the famous sommelier Luca Gardini, both designed and created by Arclinea. There will also be a Giunti Editore library with space for cultural debates and events. Ecological delivery service Green Speedy, a project by the courier Speedy Florence, works exclusively for Florence's Mercato Centrale.

The redevelopment project was designed and handled by the famous architecture studio Archea Associati of Florence under the guidance of the architect Marco Casamonti. They set themselves the target of creating a new indoor urban square, focusing on the need to equip the city center with a new contemporary meeting place. No radical regulatory and technical adjustments were necessary: the previous ones dated from 2008 and left an empty and useable space available on the first floor of the Mercato Centrale, which lacked, however, that charm and domesticity, the feeling of warmth and welcome typical of city squares. Thoughts therefore turned, rather than to invasive transformations, to

emphasised. To that end, simple and natural materials (wood, wicker, rope, terracotta, pigmented concrete) and flexible mobile furniture were used, as well as a series of large wicker and rattan lights that discretely fill the enormous market space. The architectural mix enhances the artisanal vocation of the shops. They are arranged as they would be along a street or square, in an ordered sequence which creates an open display system able to give full visibility to the processing workshops and to provide enjoyment to the public. Visitors can watch the manual activity involved in preparing the food. All the spaces of the shops, for preparation, administration and sales, along with the areas used for services, are designed to give a unitary and cheerful image of the market, albeit with each having its own specific functional characteristics," according to Marco Casamonti.

The new first floor of the Mercato Centrale creates in Florence a new destination on a European itinerary of historic food and wine markets within an architecture that combines modernity and tradition with wholly renaissance awareness. It is a work where the spirit of the past, freed from a futile sense of nostalgia and from a harmful position, becomes current and open for the city. A city where architecture, together with its history and values, will continue to be the star.

Left: The wine-tasting area and wine school by Arclinea entrusted to the famous sommelier Luca Gardini. This wine-tasting area is created with an Arclinea model designed by Antonio Citterio. Above the first floor of the Marcato Zentrale is busy from the moment it opens the doors.

Below: The Mercato Zentrale project was designed and handled by the famous architecture studio Archea Associati of Florence under the guidance of the architect Marco Casamonti, here on the right. Beside him: Fabi Silvia, Marco Casamonti, and Laura Andreini.

Next pages: The ground floor of the Mercato Centrale where the daily market is held. Right: These photo gives a good impression of how a new, ingenious grid structure has been added in the existing edifice to support the revamped first floor.

TEA-TIME TREASURES

The tea ceremony originated in China and Japan, where the preparation and drinking of tea was conducted according to all manner of rules and customs testifying to considerable refinement. The accessories themselves, which were always handled with greatest care, were considered to be revered, precious possessions. The oldest traces of tea culture in China date from the Tang dynasty (618-916 AD). The Japanese had mastered the tea ritual by the 9th century. Western explorers made mention of these intriguing tea ceremonies in their logbooks.

The first Dutch publication in which tea was mentioned dates from 1586. Jan Huygen van Linschoten noted that in Japan they had a "certaine hearbe called Chaa, which is much esteemed."
Around 1610 the first—scant—amount of tea was shipped to the Netherlands as a curiosity by the recently established Dutch East India Company (VOC). But cargo lists reveal that tea purchases were increasing considerably in the course of the 17th century. Much was intended for Dutch residents of Batavia in the Dutch East Indies, where tea consumption was adopted much sooner than in the homeland. However, when, for the first time, a large batch was unloaded in the port of Amsterdam in 1667, it sold like hot cakes—contrary to the VOC's expectations.

The first tea drinkers were mainly from the fashionable, wealthy elite who tried the exotic beverage out of curiosity. The masses were completely unfamiliar with the new drink until around 1680. But a new lucrative market had opened up for the VOC, and tea became a nomal commodity. Twenty years on and the drinking of tea had become established practice, at least among the moneyed middle classes. Yet contemporary prices suggest it must have been a prohibitively expensive luxury commodity for many. Oddly enough, in the northern—rural—provinces of the Netherlands, tea was used solely as a (soothing) medicine until around 1740, and was almost unknown as a stimulant.
By the 17th century tea drinkers had already become accustomed to adding milk and sugar to their tea.
After 1750, tea prices dropped to such an extent that everyone could afford the beverage.
Tea drinking had become so popular that around 1800 three-quarters of the Dutch beer breweries had to close down because competition was so great—all and sundry acquired the tea habit. While gentlemen amused themselves in coffee houses and clubs, convivial tea-drinking took on great social significance for ladies.

The "tea table" became a meeting-place for women who were expected to stay home. They not only partook of different kinds of tea. Sweetmeats–biscuits, chocolate, and cake–were served as well, rounded off by alcoholic beverages. Well-to-do families would have tea-houses or garden pavilions at their country villas, or else they appointed a room in their home as a "tea salon." The urge to participate in the new tea-drinking fashion resulted in the widespread purchase of expensive accessories towards the end of the 17th century.

Above: The highly decorated silver tea canister, made in Haarlem in 1718 by the silversmith Meindert Borst, is 12 cm in height. Beside it, a miniature silver tea canister, made by Arnoldus van Geffen in 1744. That Amsterdam silversmith was renowned as a maker of miniature silver items for doll's houses and for collectors of miniature wares. Height: 5.5 cm. Collection: John Endlich antiques, Haarlem, the Netherlands.

Right: Chinese cups and saucers decorated with representations of fishes, shrimps and plants. Dating from the Kangxi period–1662-1722. Saucer diameter: 13 cm, the matching cup is 5.5 cm in height. Beside that, a number of miniature cups and saucers with similar decorations, also from the Kangxi period. Diameter of the saucer: 5 cm, height of the cup: 2.8 cm. Miniature versions which today are rare, were made specially to adorn the Chinese room in a doll's house of the 18th century.

A variety of attributes used during the drinking of tea were found on and around the tea table. An 18th-century tea service comprised several pieces: not only a teapot, but also a silver or porcelain candy or sugar bowl and a pear-shaped porcelain or silver milk jug.
Costli Chinese cups and saucers, small teapots and all manner of silverware were laid out for tea-time. The tea-table itself was the focal point, with a *bouilloire* or kettle standing on a burner and used for boiling water.
Relatively small brewing pots would first be rinsed out with hot water and then used to make a strong tea extract. A small amount of the extract was poured into a porcelain cup and then diluted with hot water. Larger–sized teapots only came into use around

Previous pages:
An exceptionally large and lavishly finished 18th-century tea chest with three interior compartments in silver. The exterior (made in China) partially in carved and incised open-work mother-of-pearl. The silver components were made by the Rotterdam silversmith Rudolph Sondag in 1768. Measurements: 25 x 14.3 cm. Height, including handle: 21.5 cm.
The silver lids of the three compartments in the interior of a mother-of-pearl tea chest were decorated in Rococo style by the Rotterdam silversmith Rudolph Sondag. (Collection: John Endlich antiques, Haarlem, the Netherlands)

These pages:
Three-piece sterling silver tea set, made in 2013 by the Dutch silversmith Daan Brouwer. He entitled this unique set "Transfiguration," partly as a reference to the different techniques used in making it.
Materials: Sterling silver, gold leaf and ebony. Height of teapot and milk jug 20.5 and 11.5 cm respectively.

1900—following the English example—in which tea was made right away in the desired strength. The earliest known brewing pots were made in red stoneware. There are examples of Chinese brewing pots in existence, also pots made in Delft and Meissen. After that, small Chinese porcelain teapots imported by the VOC came into fashion. Silver teapots in all manner of shapes, types, and styles, were being made from around 1700. Tea was stored in those days in porcelain (often Chinese) or silver tea canisters—usually rectangular in shape and closed with a small round cap. The earliest and meanwhile extremely expensive silver versions date from the late 17th century.

From around 1750 onwards, tea was also kept in small chests made from costly inlaid wood, silver or tortoiseshell. Their styles varied—sometimes neoclassical Louis XVI, sometimes plainer Empire. Some tea caddies contained three copper or lead compartments: one for green tea, one for black tea, and one for a mixture of the two. Wooden or tortoiseshell chests for a single type of tea usually have an extra, lead-lined inner lid to preserve the aroma optimally. Glass and crystal tea caddies date from either the late-18th or the 19th century.

From the late-19th century, tea companies started selling tea in tins with appropriate painted or printed, often Chinese, scenes. Traditionally, tea has been drunk from a porcelain cup which stands on a saucer.

Over the years, the East India Company shipped vast numbers of cups and saucers to Europe, with either blue-and-white or polychrome decorations. As tea was relatively light compared with its volume, ballast would be added to the tea cargo for the ship's stability. The tea ships carried porcelain wares for that purpose, and also because porcelain is odourless and would not have an adverse effect on the aroma of the tea. Both Chinese and Japanese tea bowls were originally smooth and round, but in the course of the 18th century they started to be supplied with handles, at the request of Western clients, and in hexagonal or octagonal versions. As soon as craftsmen in Europe mastered the art of porcelain production, local factories emerged where tea paraphernalia could be produced.

French, Saxe and Holland porcelain, decorated in keeping with European taste, found its way to the discerning buyer. Since the wares were produced in these parts it was possible to pick up quicker on the latest fashions in color-schemes, favorite styles, and preferred illustrations. And that resulted in a waning popularity of Chinese porcelain. That is illustrated by developments beginning in the Empire period: the fashion was for custom-made, entirely white tea sets with gold decorations. The owner's initials are marked on each item with colorful depictions of buildings, landscapes, or some form of blessing for the user.

Apart from the components required specifically for tea drinking, other items came into vogue including tea boards or trays made from wood, oriental lacquerware or silver. There were also tea warmers containing a burner, used for heating the kettle.

Above: An Empire tea set, porcelain, decorated in white and gold: a wedding gift to Julius Dominicus Schulte van Haege and Henriette Elizabeth Mispelblom Beyer in 1804. The stylised initials of the bridal couple are pictured on various items including the sugar bowl, milk jug and slop basin. Height of largest item: 28.5 cm
Right: A small size Chinese Kangxi porcelain tea jar with original lid with a depiction of a Chinese lady surrounded by flowering branches. Height: 8.5 cm, c. 1690.
The late-17th century miniature silver tea caddy made in Amsterdam has a similar, rectangular shape. The porcelain miniature cups and saucers date from the Kangxi period.

In the 19th century oval mahogany serving trays with copper banding were highly popular. As were sundry smaller items used with teadrinking: silver teaspoons, sugar spoons and tongs, and tea strainers. The strainer or sieve was designed as a shallow, round or oval pierced bowl with a handle. Late 18th-century teaspoons had a wide variety of shapes: Empire models from around 1800 are elongated and have an almond-shaped bowl. On the other hand, Biedermeier spoons, made in thinner silver, often have exuberantly incised decorations. Teaspoons of that type were usually kept in teaspoon boxes with tortoiseshell veneer or applied mother-of-pearl. The silver vase-shaped spoon holder is also a typical 19th-century product. Contemporary industrial designers like Michael Graves and Philippe Starck, and design studios like Alessi do make specific designs of tea services and appurtenances, but customized tea ware for one client is rare these days. Only a true collector or design aficionado would have a unique silver tea service designed for him/her nowadays. And then it would be for the sake of possession rather than for everyday use.

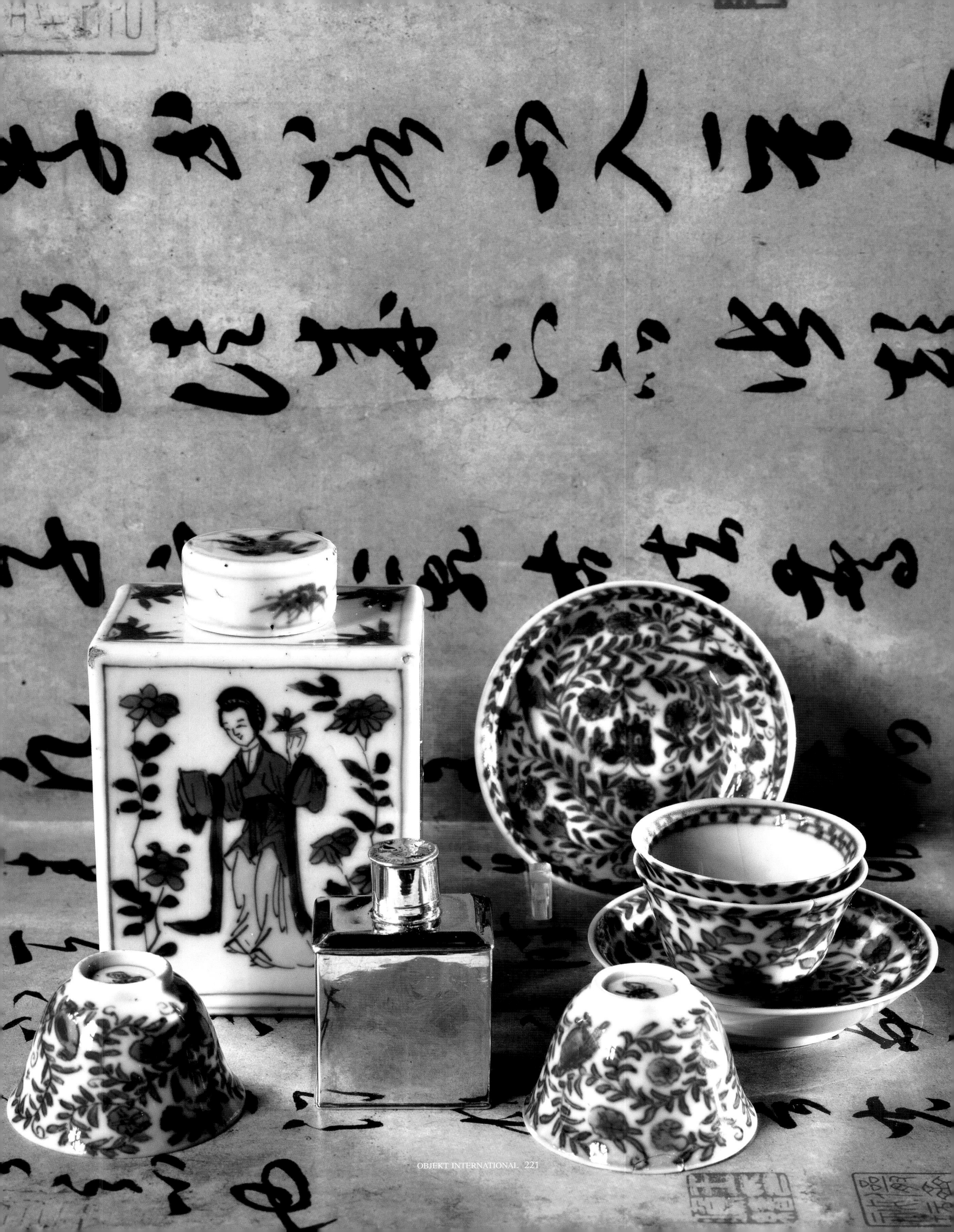

These pages: In the 17th and 18th centuries well-to-do Dutch burghers bought all manner of scaled-down silver objects, collecting them for display cabinets and doll houses.
Back left: A miniature silver tea warmer, height 6.3 cm, made by the Amsterdam silversmith Arnoldus van Geffen in 1739. Center front: a tiny, 3.2 cm, miniature teapot made by the Amsterdam silversmith Johannes A. van Geffen, 1770. He also made the miniature burner with matching *bouilloire* or kettle (1785).
Collection John Endlich Antiquair - Haarlem, the Netherlands.

IMPRINT

© 2015 teNeues Media GmbH + Co. KG, Kempen
© 2015 Objekt©International. All rights reserved.

Foreword by George M. Beylerian
Photography by Hans Fonk
Texts by Hans Fonk, Izabel Fonk
Texts China Blues and Tea-Time Treasures by
Ruud van der Neut
Text Shao Fan by Feng Hui (Cora)
Design by Hans Fonk, Alaïa Fonk

Editorial coordination by Inga Wortmann, teNeues Media
Production by Alwine Krebber, teNeues Media

Published by teNeues Publishing Group

teNeues Media GmbH + Co. KG
Am Selder 37, 47906 Kempen, Germany
Phone: +49-(0)2152-916-0
Fax: +49-(0)2152-916-111
e-mail: books@teneues.com

Press department: Andrea Rehn
Phone: +49-(0)2152-916-202
e-mail: arehn@teneues.com

teNeues Publishing Company
7 West 18th Street, New York, NY 10011, USA
Phone: +1-212-627-9090
Fax: +1-212-627-9511

teNeues Publishing UK Ltd.
12 Ferndene Road, London SE24 0AQ, UK
Phone: +44-(0)20-3542-8997

teNeues France S.A.R.L.
39, rue des Billets, 18250 Henrichemont, France
Phone: +33-(0)2-4826-9348
Fax: +33-(0)1-7072-3482

www.teneues.com

ISBN 978-3-8327-3219-6

Library of Congress Number: 2014958713

Printed in the Czech Republic

Bibliographic information published by the Deutsche Nationalbibliothek.
The Deutsche Nationalbibliothek lists this publication in the Deutsche
Nationalbibliografie; detailed bibliographic data are available in the
Internet at http://dnb.d-nb.de.

teNeues Publishing Group
Kempen
Berlin
London
Munich
New York
Paris

teNeues